MW01528144

Property of
Judy Sheridan

Q&A® 4
Quick Reference

Steven Presar

que

Q&A® 4 Quick Reference.

Library of Congress Catalog Number: 91-66192

ISBN: 0-88022-828-8

94 93 92   4 3 2

Interpretation of the printing code: the rightmost double-digit number is the year of the book's printing; the rightmost single-digit number is the number of the book's printing. For example, a printing code of 91-4 shows that the fourth printing of the book occurred in 1991.

This book is based on Q&A Version 4.

Que Quick Reference Series

The *Que Quick Reference Series* is a portable resource of essential microcomputer knowledge. Whether you are a new or experienced user, you can rely on the high-quality information contained in these convenient guides.

Drawing on the experience of many of Que's best-selling authors, the *Que Quick Reference Series* helps you easily access important program information.

The Q*ue Quick Reference Series* includes these titles:

1-2-3 Quick Reference
1-2-3 Release 2.2 Quick Reference
1-2-3 Release 2.3 Quick Reference
1-2-3 Release 3 Quick Reference
1-2-3 Release 3.1 Quick Reference
Allways Quick Reference
Assembly Language Quick Reference
AutoCAD Quick Reference, 2nd Edition
C Quick Reference
CorelDRAW Quick Reference
dBASE IV Quick Reference
DOS and BIOS Functions Quick Reference
Excel Quick Reference
Excel for Windows Quick Reference
Hard Disk Quick Reference
Harvard Graphics Quick Reference
MS-DOS 5 Quick Reference
Microsoft Word 5.5 Quick Reference
Norton Utilities Quick Reference
PC Tools Quick Reference, 2nd Edition
Q&A Quick Reference
Quattro Pro Quick Reference
QuickBASIC Quick Reference
Turbo Pascal Quick Reference
UNIX Programmer's Quick Reference
UNIX Shell Commands Quick Reference
Windows 3 Quick Reference
WordPerfect Quick Reference
WordPerfect 5.1 Quick Reference

Publisher
Lloyd J. Short

Series Director
Karen A. Bluestein

Production Editor
Laura J. Wirthlin

Technical Editor
Andrew R. Young

Production Team
Kimberly Mays, Bob LaRoche, Susan VandeWalle

Trademark Acknowledgments

1-2-3, Lotus, and Symphony are registered trademarks of Lotus Development Corporation.

Avery is a registered trademark of Avery International Corporation.

IBM Writing Assistant is a trademark and the Assistant Series is a registered trademark of International Business Machines Corporation.

Microsoft Word is a registered trademark of Microsoft Corporation.

MultiMate and Wordstar are registered trademarks of WordStar International Corporation.

PFS:Write is a trademark of Spinnaker Software Corporation.

Professional Write is a registered trademark of Software Publishing Corporation.

Q&A is a registered trademark of Symantec Corporation.

WordPerfect is a registered trademark of WordPerfect Corporation.

Table of Contents

Introduction

Q&A Quick Reference includes the quick reference information you need to work with Q&A's five modules: File, Report, Write, Intelligent Assistant, and Utilities. This book includes the reference information that you most frequently use to design and use databases, generate reports, create documents, and use Q&A's English-language data-retrieval capabilities.

Because it is a quick reference, this book is not intended to replace the extensive documentation and tutorials provided with Q&A. This book highlights the most frequently used information and reference material needed to work quickly and efficiently with Q&A. Not covered are some advanced features that few Q&A users employ, such as the program's extensive networking capabilities. (You will find, however, extensive coverage of Q&A's advanced and form programming capabilities, which are useful for virtually every Q&A user.) Moreover, this book does not attempt to teach you Q&A concepts and methods with keystroke-by-keystroke tutorials; rather, it is for review and reference.

If you are new to Q&A, there is no better way to supplement the Q&A knowledge in this book than to obtain a copy of *Using Q&A 4*, by George Beinhorn (Que Corporation, 1991). This well-written book takes you step-by-step to Q&A mastery and includes extensive coverage of advanced features such as networking and importing non-Q&A databases.

Q&A Quick Reference is divided into sections by tasks, command names, and topics. One section, for example, is *Search/Update*. This section covers procedures you use to retrieve and update forms in a File database. Additional information is found in *Search Options*, a reference section that lists codes you can use to tailor your Q&A searches.

Now you can put essential information at your fingertips with *Q&A Quick Reference*—and the entire *Que Quick Reference Series*!

Q&A Applications

Q&A includes an excellent database module, an easy-to-use report generator, a word processing module that is fully integrated with the database facilities, and a sophisticated English-language retrieval system called the Intelligent Assistant.

Q&A includes the following applications:

- **File** is a flat-file database management program. You can design your own forms, then add data to those forms to produce a database (a collection of "records," or completed forms). You can retrieve the forms you want to use and then sort, edit, update, or even delete them.

- **Report** is an easy-to-use program for printing the information in your database. You can use Q&A's built-in report formats, or you can create your own formats as easily as you create forms with File.

- **Write** is a word processing program that is fully integrated with Q&A's database capabilities. You can use Write to create letters, memos, and reports. Write includes many advanced functions such as search and replace, headers and footers, and multiple columns. You also can create reports that incorporate reports generated by File and enhance them with Lotus 1-2-3 or Symphony spreadsheets and graphics.

- **Intelligent Assistant** translates English-language queries into instructions for data retrieval and report generation. The Intelligent Assistant doesn't really understand English, though; to use the module most efficiently, you must "train" it to understand the words you use.

- **Utilities** includes facilities for importing and exporting data, installing your printer, using DOS, choosing default directories, and recovering damaged databases.

Hints for Using This Book

Because Q&A consists of five modules in one package, this *Quick Reference* includes a subheading under each command name. The subheading tells you which module to select in order to use the command. For example, the word *FILE* under Assign Access Rights tells you to select **F**ile from the Main menu in order to use the Assign Access Rights command.

Conventions used in this book

As you read this book, keep the following conventions in mind:

- All keys that you press or text that you type appears in **boldfaced blue** type.

- To select commands from menus, use the up- and down-arrow keys to highlight the command you want to use or press the letter shown in blue, as in the following example:

  Select **S**et Global Defaults from the Utilities menu.

  (Press **S** to select the **S**et Global Defaults command.)

- Q&A makes extensive use of function keys, and often uses them in combination with the **Shift**, **Ctrl**, and **Alt** keys. (You do not need to memorize the meanings of these keys.)

  Because Q&A accomplishes so many different tasks, the meaning of the function keys changes as you move among modules within the program. To help you remember the functions of these keys, many entries in this book contain summaries of the function keys for a specific command or module.

- The material in this book is extensively cross-referenced. For more information about a subject, turn to the command name or topic referenced in *italic* print, as in the following example:

  See *Information Types* for a list of information type codes.

Menu-bypassing shortcuts

Q&A's menu structure helps you navigate through the program. After you learn the structure of the program, however, you may want to use menu-bypassing shortcuts. These shortcuts bypass the menus and move from one function to another.

Key	*Result*
Adding Data	
F7	Retrieves Spec screen.
Shift-F9	Bypasses menu (Format, Restrict Spec, Initial Values Spec, Speedup Spec, Lookup Table, Help Spec, Change Palette Spec).
Updating Data	
Ctrl-F6	Adds data.
F7	Retrieves Spec screen.
Shift-F9	Bypasses menu (Format, Restrict Spec, Initial Values Spec, Speedup Spec, Lookup Table, Help Spec, Change Palette Spec).
Customizing Form Design	
Ctrl-F6	Adds data.
F7	Retrieves Spec screen.
Printing Reports	
F2	Print Options.
Shift-F9	Bypasses menu (Retrieve Spec, Column/Sort Spec, Derived Column Spec, Print Options, Define Page).

Key	Result
Printing Forms	
F2	Print Options.
Shift-F9	Bypasses menu (Retrieve Spec, Column/Sort Spec, Derived Column Spec, Print Options, Define Page).
Editing Documents	
F2	Print Options.
Alt-F8	Prints mailing labels.
Ctrl-F6	Defines page.
Shift-F8	Saves document.
Ctrl-F8	Exports document to ASCII.

COMMAND REFERENCE

The command reference is an alphabetical listing of Q&A commands and features. The name is followed by the module to select, the purpose, instructions for using the command or feature, specific function keys, and notes.

Add Data

FILE

Purpose

Displays a new, blank form for adding information to the database.

To add data

1. Select File from the Main menu.

2. Select **A**dd Data from the File menu.

3. Type the name of the data file to which you want to add data or press **Enter** to see a list of available data files.

4. Add the information. Use the **Backspace**, **Delete**, **F4**, or **Shift-F4** keys to edit text as you type.

5. Press **Tab** or **Enter** to move the cursor to the next field or use the arrow keys to navigate around the form.

6. Press **F10** to save the form and display a new form or press **Shift-F10** to save the form and exit.

   If you make a number of mistakes and prefer to start over, press **F3** and select **Y**es to delete the form permanently.

To print a displayed form

1. Press **F2** to display the File Print Options screen.

2. Select print options.

3. Press **F10** to continue.

To print all added forms

1. Press **Ctrl-Home** to select the first form.

2. Press **Ctrl-F2** to display the File Print Options screen.

3. Press **F10** to print.

Function Keys for the Add Data Command

Key	Function
F1	Displays Help screen.
F2	Prints current form.
Shift-F2	Displays Macro menu.
Ctrl-F2	Prints from current form to end of stack.

Key	Function
F3	Deletes current form.
F4	Deletes from cursor to end of field.
Shift-F4	Deletes all characters in field.
F5	Copies current field from preceding record.
Shift-F5	Copies preceding record.
Ctrl-F5	Inserts current date.
Alt-F5	Inserts current time.
F6	Activates the Field editor. Press *F10* to exit.
F7	Activates the Search/Update command.
F8	Calculates.
Shift-F8	Sets Calculation mode.
Ctrl-F8	Resets @NUMBER.
F9	Saves and displays preceding record.
Shift-F9	Displays Customize Spec screen.
F10	Saves and displays next form.
Shift-F10	Saves record and exits.
Esc	Returns to File menu.

Notes

Use Search/Update to add data to partially completed forms.

If you created a keyword field, remember to separate the keywords with semicolons.

When you design a data file, specify an information type for each field. Then, if you try to enter alphanumeric characters in a Number field, the keys you press have no effect. For other information types, Q&A checks what you entered after you exit the field. If the data entered does not conform to the specified information type, Q&A displays an error message such as `This doesn't look like a yes/no value. Please verify`. Q&A displays a similar message if you violate a Restriction Spec that you created. See *Restrict Values*.

To enter the current date in a field, press **Ctrl-F5**. To enter the current time in a field, press **Alt-F5**.

Advanced Lessons

ASSISTANT

Purpose

Teaches the Intelligent Assistant more words. [Note that Q&A 4.0 refers to this function as "Assistant" on the menu screens. Previous versions of Q&A referred to this function as the "Intelligent Assistant".]

To identify name fields

1. Select **A**ssistant from the Main menu.

2. Select **T**each Me About Your Database from the Assistant menu.

3. Select a file.

4. Press **4** to select Which Fields Contain Locations from the Basic Lessons menu.

   Or, press **6** to select Advanced Lessons from the Basic Lessons menu, then press **1** to select What fields Contain People's Names from the Advanced Lessons menu.

5. Position the cursor in the first field that contains a person's name, press **1** to identify the person, then type a code after the number to identify which part of the name the field contains.

   Use the following codes: **W**hole name, **F**irst name, **T**itle, **M**iddle name, **L**ast name, or **S**uffix (such as degree).

6. Press **Tab** to place additional codes in other fields containing this person's name.

   Each individual has one number: if you type **1L** to identify the first person's last name, type **1F** to identify the field containing that person's first name.

7. Repeat Steps 5 and 6 (with successive numbers) for each person named on the form.

8. Press **F10** to save your work and continue.

9. At the prompt, type words or phrases that describe the person whose name you identified.

10. Press **F10** again to save and continue.

To identify units of measure fields

1. Select **A**ssistant from the Main menu.

2. Select **T**each Me About Your Database from the Assistant menu.

3. Select a file.

4. Press **6** to select Advanced Lessons from the Basic Lessons menu.

5. Press **2** to select Units Of Measure from the Advanced Lessons menu.

6. Type the name of the measurement unit (if any) for the first highlighted field.

7. Press **F8** to select the next field.

8. Repeat Steps 6 and 7 until you identify all fields that contain units of measure.

9. Press **F10** to save and continue.

To teach adjectives used for comparison

1. Select **A**ssistant from the Main menu.

2. Select **T**each Me About Your Database from the Assistant menu.

3. Select a file.

4. Press **6** to select Advanced Lessons from the Basic Lessons menu.

5. Press **3** to select Advanced Vocabulary: Adjectives.

6. To use adjectives to compare the data in the first highlighted field, type the high value (such as expensive) and the low value (such as cheap).

   Do not include the comparison suffixes -er and -est.

   Intelligent Assistant knows the following bases (as well as their comparative and superlative derivatives): much, many (more, most), big (bigger, biggest), great (greater, greatest), large (larger, largest), high (higher, highest), low (lower, lowest), few (fewer, fewest), small (smaller, smallest), little (littler, littlest), less, least, above, below, under, maximum (max), minimum (min), top, and bottom.

7. Press **F8** to select the next field.

8. Repeat Steps 6 and 7 until you identify all fields that you can compare using adjectives.

9. Press **F10** to save and continue.

To teach verbs you associate with fields

1. Select **A**ssistant from the Main menu.

2. Select **T**each Me About Your Database from the **A**ssistant menu.

3. Select a file.

4. Press **6** to select Advanced Lessons from the Basic Lessons menu.

5. Press **4** to select Advanced Vocabulary: Verbs from the Advanced Lessons menu.

6. To use verbs to describe an action connected with data in the first highlighted field (such as "When was Smith hired?" or "What final grade did Jones achieve?"), type the verb.

   If the verb is irregular, you must type the irregular forms you will use.

   Intelligent Assistant knows verbs that describe the program's built-in actions, such as count, show, give, and present.

7. Press **F8** to select the next field.

8. Repeat Steps 6 and 7 until you identify all action fields.

9. Press **F10** to save and continue.

Notes

Use Advanced Lessons only after you use Basic Lessons.

Advanced Lessons choices affect the current database only.

Ask Me To Do Something

ASSISTANT

Purpose

Receives a request in English to retrieve information, add new information, change information, perform calculations, produce reports, and create synonyms.

To ask Intelligent Assistant to do something

1. Select **A** sk Me To Do Something from the Assistant menu.

2. Type the name of the database file you want to use.

3. Type the request in the Request box and press **Enter**.

   If Intelligent Assistant does not understand one of the words you typed, it asks for help. You can select to edit the word, add the word to Q&A's vocabulary, display or change the vocabulary, or ignore the problem and tell Assistant to continue.

4. Select **Y** es to confirm the request and carry out the action.

   Press **F2** to print the results of the query or command.

To add words to Intelligent Assistant's vocabulary

1. Select **A** sk Me To Do Something from the Assistant menu.

2. Type the name of the database file you want to use and press **Enter**.

3. Press **F8** to add words.

4. Indicate whether the word or phrase you want to add is a **W**ord, a **F**ield name, a **S**ynonym, a **V**erb, or **O**ther.

To change the name of Intelligent Assistant

1. Select **A**sk Me To Do Something from the Assistant menu.

2. Type the name of any database file and press **Enter**.

3. Type a new name for the Intelligent Assistant and press **Enter**.

Request Examples

Question	*Examples*
What is/are..?	What is the highest grade for Essay No. 4? What are the highest grades for Essay No. 1 and Essay No. 2?
Who..?	Who has the highest grade for Essay No. 4? Who did not hand in Essay No. 3 on time?
How Many..?	How many students handed in Essay No. 3 on time? How many students handed in 0 essays on time?
Where..?	Where did the students with above average final grades go to high school?
Show me...	Show me a list of all students whose final grade is above average, sorted by major. Show me all the forms for students who have not handed in papers on time.

Question	Examples
Get...	Get the forms for students who did not hand in Essay No. 3 on time.
Change...	Change Deborah Smith's Essay No. 3 grade from 2.75 to 3.0. Change the weight of the final exam to 15 and change the weight of Essay No. 4 to 10.
Delete...	Delete Jim Smith's form. Delete any forms with all grades blank.

Function Keys for the Ask Me To Do Something Command

Key	Function
F1	Explains how to ask.
F4	Deletes a word.
Shift-F4	Deletes a line.
F6	Displays vocabulary.
Shift-F7	Restores preceding request.
F8	Teaches words.

Notes

Use Basic Lessons and Advanced Lessons before using this command.

In general, you can ask the Intelligent Assistant to perform any database function. The examples are typical questions and commands you can use, but you may need to teach the program many additional words.

When you ask Intelligent Assistant to display data, the program displays or prints all the columns you identified in Basic Lessons. You can limit the display of data by adding the codes **WNIC** ("With No Identifying Columns"), **WNRC** ("With No Restriction Columns"), and **WNEC** ("With No Extra Columns") at the end of the query or command.

To display the data in a **Y**es/no field, you must type the word *field* after the field name.

Assign Access Rights

FILE

Purpose

Defines access privileges and passwords.

Access levels

The administrator can define the following access levels:

Administrative Rights include the right to change the Access Control screen and determine the access rights of other users.

Change Form Design enables the user to redesign and customize the database design.

Change Report Design enables the user to design or modify an existing report.

Data Access Level contains two options. The Read and Write option enables the user to add, update, or delete data. The Read Only option prevents the user from making any change to the data.

To assign access rights

1. Select **F**ile from the Main menu.

2. Select **D**esign File from the File menu.

3. Select **S**ecure A File from the Design menu.

4. Type the name of the database you want to protect and press **Enter**.

5. Select **A**ssign Access Rights from the Security menu.

6. Enter a User ID and press **Enter**.

   Enter a User ID that is easy to remember, such as the user's first name. You can include up to 20 characters.

7. Enter a password. You can include up to 10 characters. Press **Enter**.

8. Press **Tab** to select the next Access Rights field, and select the option you want to assign this user.

9. Repeat Step 8 until you finish choosing Access Rights for this user.

10. To add another user, press **Ctrl-F6** and complete the form for that user (repeat Steps 6 through 9).

    To view the forms, press **F9** to display the preceding form and **F10** to display the next form. To delete the current form, press **F3**.

11. Press **Shift-F10** to save the forms and return to the Security menu.

To change a password

1. Start Q&A and access a restricted database.

2. When the Password box appears, type your user ID and current password.

3. Press **F8** to change your password.

4. Type your User ID, then your old password, then your new password.

5. Check the password carefully and correct any errors.

6. Press **F10** to save your new password.

To delete access rights for a user

1. Select **F**ile from the Main menu.

2. Select **D**esign File from the File menu.

3. Select **S**ecure A File from the Design menu.

4. Type the name of the database you want to protect and press **Enter**.

5. Select **A**ssign Access Rights from the Security menu.

    Q&A displays the first Access Control form.

6. Use the arrow keys to highlight the user you want to delete.

7. Press **F3** to delete the form.

8. Select **Y**es and press **Esc** to return to the Security menu.

Notes

Access protection prevents unauthorized persons from reading sensitive records. The database administrator determines each user's level of access.

When the administrator defines access control, the choices affect the current database only. Other databases lack protection unless the administrator activates them and uses the Assign Access Rights command.

After a user types a User ID and password and quits Q&A, the user must enter this information when accessing the database again. The user can press F6 at the Main menu to enter the User ID and password. Alternatively, Q&A prompts for the information if the user attempts to open a restricted database.

Backup

FILE

Purpose

Creates an exact image copy of a database.

To backup a database

1. Select Utilities from the File menu.

2. Select Backup from the Utilities menu.

3. Type the name of the database you want to back up and press Enter.

4. Type the name of the destination file and press Enter.

Notes

A database consists of two files, a DTF and an IDX file. Backup copies both files.

Use Backup to make copies of your databases every time you add or update records. If your original database becomes corrupted due to a system crash, power surge, or a disk problem, you can use the backup copy.

If you want to back up a database that is larger than your floppy drive's storage capacity, use a tape backup unit, a larger-capacity floppy drive, or a backup program that can distribute a file over two or more floppies.

Backup makes an exact copy of your database, including all the gaps and other inefficiencies that occur as a database is used. To make a new working copy of your database that compacts unused space, see *Copy*.

To copy the database design without copying records, see *Copy*.

Basic Lessons

ASSISTANT

Purpose

Teaches the Intelligent Assistant information about your database.

To access the Basic Lessons menu

1. Select **A**ssistant from the Main menu.

2. Select **T**each Me About Your Database from the Assistant menu.

3. Enter the name of the database.

To teach Intelligent Assistant values for this database

1. Press **1** to select Learn Values For Assistant from the Basic Lessons menu.

2. Press **Enter**.

3. Press **F10** to save the values and continue.

To teach Intelligent Assistant what this database is about

1. Press **2** to select What This Database Is About from the Basic Lessons menu.

2. Type a word or phrase that completes the statement, "Each form contains information about a particular _____."

Type as many synonyms as you can. Press **Enter** after each synonym.

3. Press **F10** to save the words and continue.

To teach Intelligent Assistant which fields to include in reports

1. Press **3** to select Which Fields Identify A Form from the Basic Lessons menu.

2. Specify the order in which you want the fields to appear.

3. Press **F10** to save and continue.

To teach Intelligent Assistant which fields contain locations

1. Press **4** to select Which Fields Contain Locations from the Basic Lessons menu.

2. To specify the first location field you want to appear in reports, press **1**; to specify the second location field, press **2**; and so on.

    If you do not want a location field to appear, use **Tab** to skip that field.

3. Press **F10** to save and continue.

To teach Intelligent Assistant alternate field names

1. Press **5** to select Alternate Field Names from the Basic Lessons menu.

2. Type synonyms for the first field label.

    For example, you can enter the synonyms "surname," "proper name," and "last" for a field labeled "Last Name."

3. Press **F8** to select the next field.

4. Repeat Steps 2 and 3 until you identify synonyms for all the field labels.

5. Press **F10** to save and continue.

Block Operations

Purpose

Marks a block of text for copying, deleting, moving, or printing.

To copy a block of text

1. Position the cursor on the first character of the block you want to copy.

2. Press **F5** to activate highlighting.

3. Use the arrow keys to highlight the text you want to copy.

    You also can press a letter key (A-Z or a-z) to select the text up to the next occurrence of the letter.

4. Press **F10** to activate the command.

5. Move the cursor to the location where you want to copy the text.

6. Press **F10** to copy the block.

    To make another copy of the block, reposition the cursor and press **Shift-F7**.

To copy text to a new document

1. Position the cursor on the first character of the block you want to copy.

2. Press **Ctrl-F5** to activate highlighting.

3. Use the arrow keys to highlight the text you want to copy.

    You also can press a letter key (A-Z or a-z) to select all the text up to the next occurrence of the letter.

4. Press **F10** to activate the command.

5. Type the name of the new file to which you want to copy the block. Note that this command overwrites any data in an existing file.

6. Press **Enter** to copy the block to the file.

To move text within a document

1. Position the cursor on the first character of the block you want to move.

2. Press **Shift-F5** to activate highlighting.

3. Use the arrow keys to highlight all the text you want to move.

   You also can press a letter key (A-Z or a-z) to select all the text up to the next occurrence of the letter.

4. Press **F10** to activate the command.

5. Move the cursor to the location where you want to move the text.

6. Press **F10** to move the block.

   To make another copy of the block you just moved, reposition the cursor and press **Shift-F7**.

To move text to a new document

1. Position the cursor on the first character of the block you want to move.

2. Press **Alt-F5** to activate highlighting.

3. Use the arrow keys to highlight the text you want to move.

   You also can press a letter key (A-Z or a-z) to select all the text up to the next occurrence of the letter.

4. Press **F10** to activate the command.

5. Type the name of the new file to which you want to move the block. Note that this command overwrites any data in an existing file.

6. Press **Enter** to move the block to the file.

To delete a block of text

1. Position the cursor on the first character of the block you want to delete.

2. Press **F3** to activate highlighting.

3. Use the arrow keys to highlight the text you want to delete.

You also can press a letter key (A-Z or a-z) to select all the text up to the next occurrence of the letter.

4. Press **F10** to delete the block.

   To restore the deletion, press **Shift-F7** before you press any other keys.

To print a block of text

1. Turn on your printer.

2. Position the cursor on the first character of the block you want to print.

3. Press **Ctrl-F2** to activate highlighting.

4. Use the arrow keys to highlight the text you want to print.

   You also can press a letter key (A-Z or a-z) to select all the text up to the next occurrence of the letter.

5. Press **F10** to print the block.

Note

You can move text from one document to another using the Clipboard feature.

Calculations

WRITE

Purpose

Performs arithmetic and statistical operations.

To perform calculations

1. Type the numbers in a column or row using right-justified or decimal tab alignment. Do not leave blank lines between the numbers if you are performing calculations on a column.

2. Position the cursor on the last number of the column or after the last number of the row.

3. Press **Alt-F9** to display the Calculations box.

4. Select **T**otal, **A**verage, **C**ount, **M**ultiply, or **D**ivide.

    Q&A treats numbers preceded by a minus sign (–) or typed within parentheses as negative. To subtract, type a negative number and select **T**otal.

5. Position the cursor in the document where you want the result to appear.

6. Press **F10** to perform the calculation.

Note

The number of decimal places is determined by the number of decimal places in the numbers you type, except that Write adds two decimal places for averaging and division operations.

Centering a Line

FILE, WRITE

Purpose

Centers a line of text on a page.

To center a line

1. In **D**esign File or **T**ype/Edit, position the cursor in the line.

2. Press **F8** to activate the Options menu.

3. Select Align Text and press **Enter**.

4. Select Center Line and press **Enter**.

To uncenter a line

1. In **D**esign File or **T**ype/Edit, position the cursor in the line.

2. Press **F8** to activate the Options menu.

3. Select Align Text and press **Enter**.

4. Select Left or Right, then press **Enter**.

Change Palette

Purpose

Provides options for the display of foreground and background display attributes.

To view and change the palette options

1. Select **F** ile from the Main menu.

2. Select **D** esign File from the File menu.

3. Select **C** ustomize A File from the Design menu.

4. Type the name of the database you want to customize and press **Enter** .

5. Select **C** hange Palette from the Customize menu.

6. Press **F8** to see the next palette or **F6** to see the preceding palette.

   To see how text looks, you can type in the fields. Q&A does not save these characters.

7. When Q&A displays the palette you want to use, press **F10** to select the palette and return to the Customize menu.

Note

Because the choice you make is saved with the current database, you can select a distinctive palette for each database.

Checking Spelling

Purpose

Checks the current document for words that do not match Write's dictionary. Also searches for duplicated words (such as "the the").

To spell check an entire document

1. In **T**ype/Edit, press **Ctrl-Home** to position the cursor at the beginning of the document.

2. Press **Shift-F1**.

   Q&A highlights any word that does not match the dictionary and displays the Spelling menu.

3. Select an option from the Spelling menu.

4. Repeat Step 3 until Q&A displays the message `Spelling check completed.`

To check the spelling of a single word

1. Position the cursor on the word.

2. Press **Ctrl-F1**.

3. Select an option from the Spelling menu.

To edit your Personal Dictionary

1. Select **G**et from the Write menu.

2. Type the file name **qapers.dct**.

3. When Q&A displays the Import Document menu, select **A**SCII and press **Enter**.

   Although you can correct, delete, or add words, you must keep the words in alphabetical order, one per line. Enter new words in lowercase letters unless they are proper nouns.

   You must save the Personal Dictionary as ASCII text.

4. Press **Esc**.

5. Select **U**tilities.

6. Select **E**xport to ASCII.

7. Select **A**SCII.

   Or, press **Ctrl-F8** instead of using Steps 4 through 7.

8. Press **Enter**.

Spelling menu options

If Write encounters a word that does not match its dictionary, Q&A displays the Spelling menu. You can select from the following options:

- List Possible Spellings displays possible spellings of the word. You may select the word and press **Enter** to place the correct spelling in your document.

- Ignore Word & Continue skips this and all additional occurrences of the word. Select this option for seldom-used proper nouns (such as street names) and other correctly-spelled words that you do not want to add to your Personal Dictionary.

- Add To Dictionary & Continue adds the word to your Personal Dictionary and continues the spelling check. Select this option for proper nouns or technical terms that are likely to recur in your writing.

- Add To Dictionary & Stop adds the word to your Personal Dictionary and cancels the spelling check.

- Edit Word & Recheck permits you to edit the word manually. Type the correct spelling and press **Enter**. Write checks the spelling of the correction.

Clear

WRITE

Purpose

Clears the current document from memory.

To clear memory

Select **Clear** from the Write menu and press **Enter**.

If you have not saved the current document, Q&A displays a warning message. Press **N** to cancel the command or **Y** to continue.

Clipboard

WRITE

Purpose

Moves text from one document to another.

To move text from one document to another

1. Position the cursor at the beginning of the text you want to move.

   Make sure that Q&A is in the Overwrite mode. If Q&A displays `Insert` on the message line, press **Ins**.

2. Press **Shift-F5** to activate highlighting.

3. Use the arrow keys to highlight the text you want to move.

4. Press **F10** to add the text to the Clipboard.

5. Move the cursor back to the first character of the text you just added to the Clipboard, then press **F10** again.

6. Press **Shift-F8** to save the document.

7. Press **Esc** to return to the Write menu.

8. Select **G**et from the Write menu.

9. Type the name of the document to which you want to move the text. (To see a list of available documents, press the **space bar** to clear the line and press **Enter**.)

10. Press **Enter**.

11. Move the cursor to the location where you want to add the text.

12. Press **Shift-F7** to add the text.

Note

To move text within a document, see *Block Operations*.

Column/Sort Spec Codes

REPORT

Purpose

Enables advanced report features.

Column/Sort Spec Codes

Code	Explanation
A	Prints column average at bottom of column.
AB	Breaks and does subcalculations when first letter changes.
AS	Sorts in ascending order.
C	Prints count of entries at bottom of column.
C	Displays monetary amounts with commas.
CS	Cancels subcalculations.
DB	Breaks and does subcalculations when day changes.
D*n*	Uses data format *n* (type a number *n* from 1 to 20).
DS	Sorts in descending order.
H*n*	Uses time format *n* (type a number *n* from 1 to 3).
JC	Formats text center.
JL	Formats text left-justified.
JR	Formats text right-justified.
M	Formats in money format.

Code	Explanation
MAX	Prints maximum value at bottom of column.
MB	Breaks and does subcalculations when month changes.
MIN	Prints minimum value at bottom of column.
Nn	Uses n decimal places.
P	Forces new page when column break occurs.
R	Repeats values.
SA	Prints subaverages at column breaks.
SC	Prints subcounts at column breaks.
SMAX	Prints maximum value at column breaks.
SMIN	Prints minimum value at column breaks.
ST	Prints subtotals at column breaks.
T	Prints column total at bottom of column.
T	Formats as text.
TR	Truncates to fit.
U	Formats text uppercase.
WC	Displays numerical amounts without commas.
YB	Breaks and does subcalculations when year changes.

Notes

You use the Column/Sort Spec codes when you design or redesign a report format. See *Design/Redesign a Report* for details.

See *Derived Columns* for additional report calculation options.

Conditional Statements

FILE

Purpose

Executes a programming statement only if a specified condition is met.

Types of conditional statements

An IF/THEN statement executes an instruction if the condition is fulfilled. If the condition is not fulfilled, Q&A does nothing. The following is a valid IF/THEN statement:

#10: IF #4 = "Y" THEN #12 = #8 * #6

This statement says that if Field #4 contains the text "Y," then multiply the value in Field #8 by the value in Field #6 and place the result in Field #12.

An IF/THEN/ELSE statement executes the first instruction if the condition is fulfilled. If the condition is not fulfilled, Q&A executes the second instruction. The following is a valid IF/THEN/ELSE statement:

#10: IF #8 < 10 THEN #12 = 50 ELSE #12 = 100

This statement says that if Field #4 contains a value that is less than 10, then place the value 50 in Field # 12.; otherwise, place the value 100 in Field #12.

You can use the following logical operators in conditional statements to construct more complex conditions:

- AND requires that both conditions be true. The following is an IF/THEN statement that employs the AND operator:

  #10: IF #8 = "Y" AND #10 = "Y"
  THEN #12 = 100

  If Field #8 contains "Y" and Field #10 contains "Y," then place the value 100 in Field #12. The value 100 appears in Field #12 only if both conditions are true.

- OR requires that at least one condition be true. The following is an IF/THEN statement that employs the OR operator:

  #10: IF #8 = "Y" OR #10 = "Y"
  THEN #12 = 100

  If Field #8 contains "Y" or if Field #10 contains "Y," then place the value 100 in Field #12. The value 100 appears in Field #12 if either condition is true.

- NOT requires that the condition be false. The following is an IF/THEN statement that employs the NOT operator:

  #10: IF #8 = "Y" NOT #10 = "Y"
  THEN #12 = 100

  If Field #8 contains "Y" and Field #10 contains anything other than "Y," then place the value 100 in Field #12. The value 100 appears in Field #12 only if both conditions are true: Field #8 must contain "Y" and Field #10 must contain something other than "Y."

You can create multiple conditional statements within a field by linking the statements with semicolons. You also can nest conditional statements. To create multiple conditional statements, use BEGIN and END to mark the beginning of the series of statements. You also can use the left bracket ({) rather than BEGIN and the right bracket (}) rather than END. You must write a nested statement on one or more lines in sequence.

If you plan to insert complex programming statements into a field, design (or redesign) the field to be a multiple-line field. Then, you will have ample room to write the programming statement.

To create a conditional statement

1. Select **F** ile from the Main menu.

2. Select **D** esign File from the File menu.

3. Select **P** rogram A File from the Design menu.

4. Type the name of the data file you want to program, then press **Enter** .

5. Select **P** rogram Form from the Programming menu.

   Q&A displays the Program Spec screen.

6. Add field ID numbers to any fields you need to reference in your statement.

   Type the field ID number (such as **#110**), then a colon (**:**).

   See *Field ID Number* for more information.

7. Position the cursor in the field where you want the conditional statement to appear.

8. Type the IF/THEN or IF/THEN/ELSE statement.

   Follow the preceding examples carefully to make sure that you use the correct syntax.

9. Press **F10** to save your statement and return to the File menu.

Notes

You create conditional statements the same way you create other statements; see *Programming Statements* for information.

Copy

Purpose

Creates a new database using the database design, the data, and the instructions you gave Intelligent Assistant.

Types of copies

You can copy your database in three ways:

- Copy **D**esign Only copies the form design and all customizing options you have chosen, but does not copy data records or Intelligent Assistant information. If you have not used Intelligent Assistant, select this option.

- Copy Design With **I**A/QG copies the form design, all customizing options you have chosen, and the information you have taught Intelligent Assistant about the database.

- Copy **S**elected Records by first copying the form design to create the destination database (so that the destination database's form design is exactly the same as the source database's form design). You then use a procedure similar to **S**earch/Update to retrieve the forms you want to copy to the new database. You can sort the source database so that the records in the destination database appear in sorted order.

To copy the design only

1. Select **C**opy from the File menu.

2. Type the name of the database.

   To see a list of available databases, press the **space bar** to clear the line and press **Enter**.

3. Select Copy **D**esign Only.

4. Type a new database name.

5. Press **Enter**.

To copy the design with Intelligent Assistant information

1. Select **C**opy from the File menu.

2. Type the name of the database.

   To see a list of available databases, press the **space bar** to clear the line and press **Enter**.

3. Select Copy Design with **I**A/QG.

4. Type a new database name.

5. Press **Enter**.

To copy selected or sorted data records from one database to another

1. Use one of the preceding procedures to copy the database design.

2. Select **C**opy from the File menu.

3. Type the name of the database from which you are copying and press **Enter**.

4. Select Copy **S**elected Records.

5. Type the name of the database to which you are copying and press **Enter**.

   Q&A displays a Retrieve Spec screen.

6. Use the Retrieve Spec screen to select the records you want to copy. (You also can retrieve records based on criteria you specify.)

   You can sort the records by pressing **F8**.

   After you sort or retrieve the records, Q&A displays the Merge Spec screen.

7. Press **F10** to copy all the fields in the order they appear on-screen.

To copy selected data fields to a new database design

1. Use the preceding procedure to create a new database containing selected fields from the source database. The field names, information types, and formats must match the corresponding fields from the source database.

2. Select **A**dd Data from the File menu to display the new form.

3. Type the name of the new database file.

4. Press **F2** and then **F10** to print a copy of the new form. (Use this copy to assist you as you copy the fields.)

5. Press **Esc** to return to the File menu.

6. Select **C**opy.

7. Type the name of the database from which you are copying and press **Enter**.

8. Select Copy **S**elected Records.

9. Type the name of the database to which you are copying and press **Enter**.

    Q&A displays a Retrieve Spec screen.

10. Use the Retrieve Spec screen to retrieve the records you want to copy. Press **F10** to retrieve all the records or use selection criteria to retrieve just some of the records.

    You can sort the records by pressing **F8**.

    After you sort or retrieve the records, Q&A displays the Merge Spec screen.

11. Enter numbers in the Merge Spec fields that correspond exactly to the order in which the fields appear in the destination database.

    If the first field of the destination database is Last Name, for example, type **1** in the Last Name field.

12. Press **F10** to start copying the fields.

Notes

To make an exact backup copy of your database for security, the **B**ackup option is faster than **C**opy. Use **C**opy if you want to copy the database design, the database design and selected records, or some but not all of the fields.

A frequently used database can become less efficient in use of disk space and retrieval time. When you use **B**ackup, Q&A makes an exact copy of the original— including the gaps and inefficient arrangements that fill disk space and slow retrieval time. When you copy all the records with **C**opy, however, Q&A creates a more efficient version of the database.

To copy forms, copy from the source database to the destination database.

Copy a Document

WRITE

Purpose

Creates a backup copy of a Write document.

To copy a document

1. Select **W**rite from the Main menu.

2. Select **U**tilities from the Write menu.

3. Select **D**OS Facilities from the Utilities menu.

4. Select **C**opy A Document from the DOS Facilities menu.

5. Type the name of the document you want to copy.

6. Press **Enter**.

7. Type the name of the backup document.

8. Press **Enter**.

Counting

WRITE

Purpose

Counts the number of words, lines, and paragraphs in a document.

To count words, lines, and paragraphs
From **T**ype/Edit, press **Ctrl-F3**.

Cursor Movement

FILE, WRITE

Purpose

Moves the cursor around the screen and from screen to screen.

Cursor-Movement Keys

Key	*Cursor Effect*
Up arrow	Moves up one line or field.
Down arrow	Moves down one line or field.
Right arrow	Moves right one character.
Left arrow	Moves left one character.
Ctrl-Right arrow	Moves right one word.
Ctrl-Left arrow	Moves left one word.
Tab	Moves to next field (File).
Shift-Tab	Moves to preceding field (File).
PgUp	Moves to first character of preceding screen.
PgDn	Moves to first character of next screen.
Ctrl-PgUp	Moves to first character of preceding page (Write).
Ctrl-PgDn	Moves to first character of next page (Write).

Key	Cursor Effect
Home	Moves to first character of line.
End	Moves to last character of line.
Home Home	Moves to first character of current page.
End End	Moves to last character of current page.
Ctrl-Home	Moves to first character of form (File) or document (Write).
Ctrl-End	Moves to last character of form (File) or document (Write).
Home Home Home	Moves to first character of form (File) or page (Write).
End End End	Moves to last character of form (File) or page (Write).
Home Home Home Home	Moves to first character of document (Write).
End End End End	Moves to last character of document (Write).
F9	Scrolls up (Write).
Shift-F9	Scrolls down (Write).
Ctrl-F7	Goes to specified page or line.

Cursor-Movement Commands

FILE

Purpose

Automates cursor movement as you move from field to field in a form.

To create a cursor-movement command

1. Select **F**ile from the Main menu.

2. Select **D**esign File from the File menu.

3. Select **P**rogram A File from the Design menu.

4. Type the name of the database you want to program and press **Enter**.

5. Select Field **N**avigation from the Programming menu.

6. If you plan to use the GOTO cursor-movement command, enter field ID numbers in all fields to be referenced by programming statements. Press the pound sign (**#**) and then a unique whole number to identify the field.

7. Enter the cursor-movement command in the field.

   To execute the statement when you move the cursor into the field, begin the statement with a less-than sign (**<**). To execute the statement when you move the cursor out of the field, begin the statement with a greater-than sign (**>**). Normally, use the greater-than sign.

   If the formula is too long to fit in the field, press **F6** to expand the field temporarily, then continue typing the statement. Press **Tab** to exit the expanded field window.

8. Repeat Steps 6 and 7 to write additional cursor-movement commands.

9. Press **F10** to save your programming statements and return to the **F**ile menu.

Cursor-Movement Commands

Command	Effect
CEND	Moves the cursor to the last field in the form.
CHOME	Moves the cursor to the first field in the form.

Command	Effect
CNEXT	Moves the cursor to the next field in the form.
CPREV	Moves the cursor to the preceding field in the form.
GOTO *field ID#*	Moves the cursor to the field whose ID# matches the number in the statement.
PgDn	Moves the cursor to the first field on the next page.
PgUp	Moves the cursor to the first field on the preceding page.

Note

Cursor-movement commands are programming statements that you create by choosing Program A File from the Customize menu. The statements affect all records in the database when you add or update records.

Customize a File

FILE

Purpose

Provides database customizing options.

To access the Customize menu

1. Select File from the Main menu.

2. Select Design File from the File menu.

3. Select Customize A File.

4. Type the name of the database you want to customize.

    To see a list of available databases, press the space bar to clear the line and press Enter.

5. Press Enter.

Customization options

You can customize a file in the following ways:

- Change the Format Options or information types. See *Format Values*.

- Place further restrictions on what you can type in a field. See *Restrict Values*.

- Set field templates to help data entry and to help control how the information is formatted.

- Insert default (most likely) values into a field to save time in data entry. See *Set Initial Values*.

- Index the fields you commonly search so that searches proceed more quickly. See *Speed Up Searches*.

- Display a customized Help menu to assist data entry on a field-by-information-blank basis. See *Define Custom Help*.

- Select colors, shading, and underlining to make your form stand out. See *Change Palette*.

Date and Time Display

FILE, REPORT

Purpose

Sets formats for display of dates and times in data records and reports.

Date Display Formats

Code	Date Display Format
1	Jul 12, 1990
2	12 Jul 1990
3	7/12/90
4	12/7/90

Code	Date Display Format
5	7/12/1990
6	12/7/1990
7	07/12/90
8	12/07/90
9	07/12/1990
10	12/07/1990
11	July 12, 1990
12	12 July 1990
13	7-12-90
14	7-12-1990
15	07-12-90
16	07-12-1990
17	12.07.90
18	12.07.1990
19	1990-07-12
20	1990/07/12

Time Display Formats

Code	Time Display Formats
1	3:50 p.m.
2	15:50
3	15.50

Define Custom Help

FILE

Purpose

Creates a custom Help box that appears on-screen.

To create a custom Help box

1. Select File from the Main menu.

2. Select Design File from the File menu.

3. Select Customize A File from the Design menu.

4. Type the name of the database you want to customize. Press Enter.

5. Select Define Custom Help from the Customize menu.

   Q&A displays the Help Spec screen. The cursor is positioned in the first field. To select other fields, press F8 to select the next field or F6 to select the preceding field.

6. Type the help message for that field.

7. To type another message, press F6 or F8 to select another field for which you want to create a Help box.

8. Repeat Steps 6 and 7 to add more Help boxes.

9. Press F10 to save your Help boxes and return to the Customize menu.

To tell the user that Help boxes are available

1. Select Program Form from the Customize menu.

2. Type the following statement in each field to which you added a Help statement. Use new field ID numbers.

   Field ID#:@msg"Press F1 to see a Help box for this field."

   Make sure that you enclose the message in quotation marks.

3. Press **F10**.

To use a Help box

1. Position the cursor in the field.

2. Press **F1**.

3. To quit the Help box, press **Esc**.

Define Page

Purpose

Defines page size, margins, characters per inch, page numbering, and headers/footers for database output.

To add page numbers in a header or footer

1. Select **R**eport from the Main menu.

2. Select **S**et Global Options from the Report menu.

3. Type the name of the file and select **C**olumnar Global Options.

4. Select Set Page Options (**D**) from the Columnar Global Options menu.

5. In the Define Page screen, press **Tab** to select the Header or the Footer area.

6. Use the cursor-movement keys to position the cursor where you want the page number to appear.

   Although you can create a header of up to three lines, most headers and footers use only one line (the first).

7. Press the pound sign (**#**).

To include date and time in a header or footer

1. In the Define Page screen, press **Tab** to select the Header or the Footer area.

2. Use the cursor-movement keys to position the cursor where you want the date or time to appear.

Although you can create a header of three lines, most headers and footers use only one line.

3. Type the code to display the date or time.

You can type both codes on the same line (and include page numbers).

To create a three-part header or footer

1. Position the cursor in the first column of one of the lines in the Header or the Footer area.

2. Type the text or the code you want to print left-justified.

Omit this step if you don't want to print anything left-justified.

3. Type an exclamation point (!).

4. Type the text or the code you want to center.

5. Type another exclamation point (!).

6. Type the text or the code you want to print right-justified.

Omit this step if you don't want to print anything right-justified.

Define Page defaults

Q&A uses the following defaults, which appear on the Define Page screen:

- **Page Width:** 85 character columns (spaces).

- **Page Length:** 66 lines.

- **Left Margin:** 5 character columns.

- **Right Margin:** 80 character columns from the left edge of the page.

- **Top Margin:** 3 lines.

- **Bottom Margin:** 3 lines.

- **Characters per Inch:** 10 cpi (Pica).

You also can select 12 cpi (Elite); 15 cpi (compressed printing on a daisywheel printer); or 17 cpi (compressed printing on a dot-matrix printer).

- **Header:** blank.

- **Footer:** blank.

Notes

You can define page options when you create a Print Spec or report format for a database (see *Design/Redesign a Spec* and *Design/Redesign a Report*). The page options you select affect that Print Spec or report format only.

You also can select new default page options that affect all new Print Specs or report formats by choosing the Set Global Options command in the File or Report modules.

Define Page

WRITE

Purpose

Defines the page size, margins, characters per inch, and the page on which Write starts printing page numbers and headers and footers.

To change the margins for the whole document

1. In Type/Edit, press Ctrl-F6.

2. Enter a new measurement for the left margin. (You can enter the number of inches or columns.)

3. Press Tab.

4. Enter a new measurement for the right margin.

   To enter the measurement in columns, enter the number of columns from the left edge of the page. To enter the measurement in inches, enter the number of inches from the right edge of the page.

5. Press Tab.

6. Enter the number of inches or lines for the top margin, measured from the top.

7. Press **Tab**.

8. Enter the number of inches or lines for the bottom margin, measured from the bottom.

9. Press **F10** to continue.

To suppress page numbers and headers on Page 1 of a document

1. In **T**ype/Edit, press **Ctrl-F6**.

2. Press **Tab** to select Begin Header/Footer On Page #:, and type the page number on which you want headers or footers to begin.

3. Press **Tab** to select Begin Page Numbering With Page #:, and type the page number on which you want page numbering to begin.

4. Press **F10** to continue.

Define Page defaults

Q&A uses the following defaults, which are shown in the Define Page screen:

- **Left Margin:** 10 character columns (one inch).

- **Right Margin:** 68 character columns from the left edge of the page.

- **Top Margin:** 6 lines.

- **Bottom Margin:** 6 lines.

- **Page Width:** 78 character columns.

- **Page Length:** 66 lines.

- **Characters per Inch:** 10 cpi (Pica).

  You also can select 12 cpi (Elite), 15 cpi (compressed printing on a daisywheel printer), or 17 cpi (compressed printing on a dot-matrix printer).

- **Begin header/footer on page #:** 1.

- **Begin page numbering on page #:** 1.

Notes

You can define page options when you create and save a document (see *Type/Edit*). The page options you select affect that Print Spec or report format only.

The choices you make on the Define Page screen affect the current document. You also can select new default page options for all new documents you create with Write. For more information, see *Set Global Options (WRITE)*.

To add headers or footers (including page numbers) to a Write document, see *Edit Header/Edit Footer*.

To change the margins within a document temporarily, see *Temporary Margins*.

Delete

ASSISTANT, FILE, REPORT, WRITE

Purpose

Deletes characters, words, and blocks in text editing; deletes records in Search/Update (File).

To delete a form in the File module

1. Select Search/Update from the File menu.

2. Type the name of the database containing the form you want to delete and press **Enter**.

3. Use the Retrieve Spec screen to limit the search to the form you want to delete.

4. Press **F10** to display the form.

5. Press **F3** to delete the form.

6. Select **Y**es to confirm the deletion.

To delete a block of text in the Write module

1. Position the cursor on the first character of the block you want to delete.

2. Press **F3** to activate highlighting.

3. Use the arrow keys to highlight the text you want to delete.

   You also can press a letter key (A-Z or a-z) to select all text up to the next occurrence of the letter that you press.

4. Press **F10** to delete.

   To restore the deleted text, press **Shift-F7** before doing anything else.

To delete a document in the Write module

1. Select **W** rite from the Main menu.

2. Select **U** tilities from the Write menu.

3. Select **D** OS Facilities from the Utilities menu.

4. Select **D** elete A Document from the DOS Facilities menu.

5. Type the file name of the document you want to delete. Press **Enter** to delete the document.

6. Select **Y** es to confirm the deletion.

Deletion Keys

Key	Effect
Backspace	Deletes one character to the left of the cursor.
Del	Deletes the character on which the cursor is positioned.
F4	Deletes the word in which the cursor is positioned.
Shift-F4	Deletes all characters in a field (File) or line (Write).
Shift-F7	Restores deletion.
F3	Deletes block (Write).

Note

> To restore words, lines, or blocks you just deleted, press **Shift-F7** before doing anything else. You cannot undelete text you deleted with the **Backspace** or **Del** keys.

Derived Columns

Purpose

> Produces reports using information not directly available from fields of the data records.

To create a derived column

1. Select **R**eport from the Main menu.

2. Select **D**esign/Redesign A Report from the Report menu.

3. Type the name of the data file for which you are designing the report.

4. Press **Enter**.

5. Type a name for the report format and press **Enter**. You can use up to 31 characters in the name.

6. Select the records you want to print with the Retrieve Spec screen.

   To print all the records, press **F10**.

   For more information on selecting records, see *Search/Update* and *Search Options*.

7. When Q&A displays the Column/Sort Spec screen, type a number from 1 through 50 in the fields you want to list as columns. Add additional codes separated by commas to indicate how you want to sort and total the data. If you run out of room, press **F6** to expand the line.

   For a list of codes, see *Column/Sort Spec Codes*.

8. After you number the columns you want to print, make a note of the column numbers you need to reference in your derived column calculations.

   For instance, if you want to print a derived column that shows the result of SALES (Column 2) times COMMISSION RATE (Column 3), note these two column numbers.

9. Press F8 to display the Derived Columns screen.

10. In the first Heading field, type the derived column's heading.

11. In the Formula field, type a formula that refers to the column numbers you used in the Column/Sort Spec screen.

    To multiply Column 2 by Column 3, for example, type #2*#3.

12. In the Column Spec field, type the number of the column in which you want the derived figures to appear.

    Use a number you did not use on the Column/Sort Spec screen.

13. Repeat Steps 10 through 12 for additional derived columns.

14. Press F10 to display the Report Print Options screen.

15. Select print options, then press F10.

16. Select Yes to print the report or No to return to the Report menu.

Notes

When you produce a report, Q&A can sort the data and perform operations such as subtotals, totals, and averages.

You can add columns to a report in which Q&A prints derived data. Derived data is generated by performing calculations on existing data fields in ways that are not included in the form design. For example, a form lists an employee's monthly salary and the number of tax exemptions claimed, but it does not compute the amount of tax to be withheld. This computation can be accomplished with a derived column.

When you define a derived column, you write a formula to tell Q&A to compute figures listed in regular report columns. You can use Operators and column ID numbers. Be careful to observe rules of precedence (see *Operators*) and use parentheses if necessary.

In the formulas you create, you can use Summary functions that reference the totals and subtotals of other columns in the report. You also can use the Lookup functions, @LOOKUP, @LOOKUPR, @XLOOKUP, and @XLOOKUPR. See *Lookup Statements*, *External Lookup Statements*, and *Functions* for further information.

Design File

FILE

Purpose

Creates the form design (and a new database).

To design a new file

1. Select **F**ile from the Main menu.

2. Select **D**esign File from the File menu.

3. Select **D**esign A New File from the Design menu.

4. Type the file name.

5. Press **F8** to display the Options screen so that you can draw lines or boxes or set new tabs before you add fields.

   To set tabs, select Set Tabs. See *Tabs* for more information. To add lines or boxes, select Draw. See *Draw* for more information.

   Press **F10** when you finish using these options.

6. Position the cursor where you want a field to appear.

7. Type the field label followed by a colon (:).

   If you want to limit the field length to a number of characters you specify, insert that number of spaces by pressing the space bar. Then type a greater-than symbol (>).

   If you plan to insert complex programming statements into a field, create a multiple-line field. Press Enter to leave blank lines. Then press Tab to move the cursor to the right edge of the form, and type a greater-than symbol (>).

   Or, press F6 in the Program Spec screen to expand the field. You then have room to write the programming statement. For more information, see *Programming Statements*.

8. Press Tab or use the arrow keys to move to the next field's location.

9. Repeat Steps 6 through 8 until you enter all the fields.

10. Press F10.

11. Select the information type and format options for each field.

    The default information type is Text, and the default format option is Justify Left.

12. Press F10.

    If you select a Dates, Hours, Number, or Money information type, Q&A displays the Global Format Options screen. You can change the global formats for these fields, or press F10 to continue.

To center a line

1. Position the cursor in the line you want to center.

2. Press F8 to display the Options screen.

3. Select Align text.

4. Select Center.

To create a rectangular field

1. When you finish typing the label, type a less-than symbol (<) rather than a colon (:).

2. Press **Enter** to leave blank lines.

3. Press **Tab** to position the cursor at the right edge of the form.

4. Type a greater-than symbol (>) to mark the end of the field.

Function Keys for the Design File Command

Key	Function
F1	Provides Help.
Shift-F2	Macro menu.
F3	Deletes block.
Ctrl-F3	Counts words, lines, and paragraphs.
F4	Deletes from cursor to end of field.
Shift-F4	Deletes all characters in field.
F5	Copies a block.
Shift-F5	Moves a block.
Ctrl-F5	Copies a block to a file.
Alt-F5	Moves a block to a file.
Alt-F6	Inserts a soft hyphen.
F7	Searches and replaces.
Shift-F7	Restores deletion.
Ctrl-F7	Displays Go To menu.
F8	Displays Options menu.
Shift-F8	Sets Calculation mode.

Key	Function
Ctrl-F8	Resets @NUMBER.
F10	Saves form design.

Notes

To create a Q&A database, you begin by choosing the **D**esign File command. This command enables you to specify where you want data fields to appear. You can arrange the fields and type the labels as if you were using a word processing program.

A Q&A form includes labels and fields. When you create the form, you lay out the labels using the tools available in Write (and can add lines or boxes using Draw). You also assign information types to each field. The information type specifies what kind of data the user can type in the field. In addition,you can select format options (such as right-justified alignment). Finally, if you chose **N**umber, **M**oney, **H**ours, or **D**ates information types, you select global format options for the display of this information.

You can create a form that occupies up to 10 screens in length and a field that takes up an entire screen.

You also can center lines and create rectangular fields. A rectangular field is a multiline field in which the second (turnover) lines are indented to align with the label. This alignment makes data entry easier and helps make the form easier to read, although you cannot draw boxes around multiline fields.

You can select additional options by customizing the file (see *Customize a File*).

Design/Redesign a Report

REPORT

Purpose

Creates or updates a report format.

To create a report format

1. Select R eport from the Main menu.

2. Select D esign/Redesign A Report.

3. Type the name of the database for which you are designing the report.

4. Press Enter .

5. Type a name for the report format and press Enter . You can use up to 31 characters in the name.

6. Select the records you want to print with the Retrieve Spec screen.

   To print all the records, press F10 .

   For more information on selecting records, see *Search/Update* and *Search Options*.

7. When Q&A displays the Column/Sort Spec screen, type a number from 1 through 50 in the fields you want to list as columns. Add additional codes to indicate how you want to sort and total the data. Be sure to separate each code with a comma. If you run out of room, press F6 to expand the line.

   For a list of codes, see *Column/Sort Spec Codes*.

   Press F8 to create derived columns.

8. Press F10 to display the Report Print Options screen.

9. Select print options.

   See *Print Options (FILE, REPORT)* for more information on this screen's options.

   To change the page definition for this report format only, press F8 and select new settings for margins, page size, characters per inch, headers, and footers from the Define Page screen. For more information on these options, see *Define Page (FILE, REPORT)*. To change the page definition settings for all new report formats, see *Set Global Options (REPORT)* .

10. Select Y es to print the report or N o to return to the R eport menu.

To redesign a report format

1. Select Report from the Main menu.

2. Select Design/Redesign A Report.

3. Type the name of the database for which you are designing the report.

4. Press Enter.

5. Highlight the name of the report format and press Enter.

6. Select the records you want to print with the Retrieve Spec screen.

   To print all the records, press F10.

   For more information on selecting records, see *Search/Update* and *Search Options*.

7. When Q&A displays the Column/Sort Spec screen, make any changes to the report format.

8. Press F10 to display the Report Print Options screen.

9. Select print options, then press F10.

10. Select Yes to print the report or No to return to the Report menu.

Column/Sort Spec Function Keys

Key	Function
F1	Provides Help.
Shift-F2	Displays Macro menu.
F3	Deletes all specs.
F4	Deletes word.
Shift-F4	Deletes all characters in field.
Ctrl-F5	Enters current date.
Alt-F5	Enters current time.
F8	Displays Derived Columns screen.

Key	Function
F9	Returns to Retrieve Spec screen.
F10	Saves Column/Sort Specs and continues.

Notes

In contrast to the Print command in the File menu, which prints data record-by-record, the Report commands generate columnar output. Because Report has so many options, you must create a report format that records your print output choices.

When you use Design/Redesign A Report, Q&A displays the Column/Sort Spec screen, which looks exactly like the Retrieval Spec screen. You type codes in the fields of this screen to determine which fields appear in columns and how Q&A should sort your output. For a list of codes, see *Column/Sort Spec Codes*.

If you type more than one code, separate the codes with commas. The following are some valid Column/Sort Spec codes and explanations of what they do:

Code	Explanation
1, AS, AB	Sorts the data in the field in ascending order (AS), and prints this field in the first column (1). Breaks the column (AB) when the first letter changes.
3, ST, T	Prints the data in this field in the third column (3), and prints subtotals (ST) at every column break. Prints totals (T) at the bottom of the column.

Design/Redesign a Spec

FILE

Purpose

Formats database output for simple free-form or coordinate printing.

Styles of printing

When you use the **D**esign/Redesign a Spec command,
Q&A displays the Print Spec screen. Q&A offers the
following styles of printing:

- Use **free-form codes** for simple printouts that lack
  formatting such as headers and footers. You can
  specify which fields you want to print and in what
  order. You also can control spacing between fields
  and insert blank lines.

- Use **co-ordinate codes** to specify exactly where on
  the page you want information to appear. Use this
  option to print on preprinted forms.

You cannot combine free-form codes and co-ordinate
codes in a Print Spec; you must select between them.

Free-form codes

The free-form codes enable you to indicate which fields
to print and the order in which they appear on the
printout. You can add blank spaces, start new lines, and
indicate the maximum number of characters to print
from the field.

- Use a number from 1 to 999 to indicate which fields
  you want to print and in what order you want them to
  appear on the printout.

- After the number, press **x** (start a new line after
  printing the field) or **+** (skip a space after printing the
  field). To tell Q&A to skip additional spaces or lines
  after the field, enter a comma after the **x** or **+**, and
  then type the number of additional spaces or lines you
  want to skip.

- Type a comma and a number indicating the
  maximum number of characters to print. Use this
  feature to make sure that a long entry does not
  exceed the line length and cause printing problems.

The following are examples of correct free-form codes:

Code	Explanation
3x	Makes this field the third to print, then starts a new line.

Code	Explanation
1+	First field, then one blank space.
1+,5	First field, then five blank spaces.
3x,2	Third field, then two blank lines.
5x,2,25	Fifth field, then two blank lines (25 characters maximum).
5x,,25	Fifth field, 25 characters maximum (note that two commas are needed).

You can use free-form reports for mailing labels, but using the Mailing Label menu in Write is easier.

Co-ordinate codes

The co-ordinate codes enable you to specify where fields print on the page. This feature is useful for printing on preprinted business forms. If you type co-ordinates into a field, the field prints. (Blank fields do not print.) Type the following, separated by commas:

- **Line Number:** A page has 66 lines (6 lines per inch). Line 6 is one inch from the top of the page.

- **Column Number:** A standard 8 1/2-wide page has 85 character positions, assuming a standard Pica font.

- **Maximum Number of Characters:** (optional) Type a number to indicate the maximum number of characters to print.

The following codes are examples of correct co-ordinate codes:

Code	Explanation
6,10	Begin field six lines from top, 10 spaces from left.
6, 25,25	Begin field six lines from top, 25 spaces from left, 25 characters maximum.

See *Rename/Delete/Copy a Spec* for information on renaming, deleting, or copying Print Specs.

To display the Print Spec screen

1. Select **F**ile from the Main menu.

2. Select **P**rint from the File menu.

3. Type the name of the database for which you want to design or redesign a Print Spec.

   Q&A displays the Print menu. Select **D**esign/ Redesign a Spec. Press **Enter**.

   Q&A displays a list of the Print Specs you created for this database. If you did not create any Print Specs, the screen is blank.

4. Type the Print Spec name and press **Enter**.

   If you create a new Print Spec, you can use up to 30 characters; you do not need to obey DOS conventions.

   You now see the Retrieve Spec screen.

5. Retrieve the records you want to print.

   If you want to print the entire database, press **F10** without specifying any search criteria.

   See *Sort* for more information. See *Search/Update* for information on retrieving records.

   After you retrieve the records, Q&A displays the Fields Spec screen.

6. Type field specs to indicate what information prints.

   To print all the fields on the form (as displayed on the form design), press **F10**.

   If you want to print some of the fields, select between free-form and co-ordinate codes. Type the codes in the fields you want to print. Then press **F10**.

7. Select print options.

   Or, press **F8** to select page definition options for this Print Spec only. See *Define Page (FILE, REPORT)* for a list of these options, including headers and footers with page numbers, date and time, and centered text. Press **F9** to return to the File Print Options screen.

8. Press **F10** to save and continue.

9. Press **Enter** to print the forms.

Notes

In contrast to the **P**rint command in the File menu, which produces simple output, the **D**esign/Redesign a Spec command enables you to specify which fields print, and in what order they print. You also can control where the fields appear on-screen.

Before creating a Print Spec, see *Set Global Options (FILE)* for information on choosing Print Spec defaults. This command affects new Print Specs only, so make these choices before creating a Print Spec.

Ditto

FILE

Purpose

Copies data from a field in the preceding form to the same field on a new, blank form. You also can copy all the data on a previously-viewed form to all the fields on a new, blank form.

To copy information from a field on the preceding form

1. Position the cursor in the field to which you want to copy the information.

2. Press **F5** to copy the data.

To copy the previously viewed form

1. Display the form using **S**earch/Update.

2. Exit **S**earch/Update and select **A**dd Data from the File menu.

3. Press **Shift-F5** to copy the form.

Notes

Use this time-saving command when you enter the same information (such as a state or zip code) on many forms.

You cannot use Ditto if you just pressed **F9** or **F10** to move between forms.

Draw

Purpose

Adds lines or boxes to a form or document.

To add lines or boxes to a form or document

1. Position the cursor where you want the line or box to begin.

2. Press **F8** (Options).

3. Select Lay Out Page, then select Draw.

4. Press one of the keys on the numeric keypad to begin drawing.

    Hold down the **Shift** key to draw a double line. To lock on double lines, press **Num Lock**.

    To stop drawing and move the cursor to a new location, press **F6** to lift up the pen. Then press **F6** to lower the pen again.

    To erase a line, press **F8**. Then press **F8** again to resume drawing.

5. Press **F10** when you finish drawing.

Cursor-Movement Keys for the Draw Command

Key	Draws line
Up arrow	Up.
PgUp	Diagonally up and right.
Right arrow	Right.
PgDn	Diagonally down and right.
Down arrow	Down.

Key	Draws line
End	Diagonally down and left.
Left arrow	Left.
Home	Diagonally up and left.

Function Keys for the Draw Command

Key	Function
F6	Pen up/pen down.
F8	Erase.
F10	Exit Draw and resume editing.

Notes

Even though you can display lines and boxes on your screen, your printer may not be able to print them. To find out whether your printer can print lines and boxes, create a new document, add a box, then try to print the document.

You can create single lines and double lines.

The lines and boxes you add are composed of ordinary on-screen characters, which can be deleted or moved. After you create a line or box, be careful as you type to avoid disturbing these characters. Keep Insert mode off as you type so that Q&A does not push the lines or boxes aside to make room for the text you type.

Edit Header/Edit Footer

WRITE

Purpose

Creates a header or footer for your document.

To create a header or footer

1. Press **Ctrl-F8**.

2. Select Edit Header or Edit Footer from the Options menu.

3. Type the header or footer text in the window.

   To include the page number, type a pound sign (#).

   To include the current time, type *@TIME(*n*)*, where *n* is one of the time codes (see *Date and Time Display*).

   To include the current date, type *@DATE(*n*)*, where *n* is one of the date codes (see *Date and Time Display*).

4. Press F10.

Notes

For information on creating headers or footers for database reports, see *Design/Redesign a Spec, Design/ Redesign a Report,* and *Define Page (FILE, REPORT)*.

To suppress the printing of headers or footers on the first page of a document, see *Define Page (WRITE)*.

Edit Lookup Table

FILE

Purpose

Creates a lookup table or enables editing of the current data file's lookup table.

To create or edit a lookup table

1. Select File from the Main menu.

2. Select Design File from the File menu.

3. Select Program A File from the Design menu.

4. Type the name of the database you want to program.

   To see a list of available databases, press the space bar to clear the line and press Enter.

5. Select Edit Lookup Table from the Programming menu.

Q&A displays the Lookup Table screen for the current database.

6. Type the key values in the Key column.

7. Type the corresponding values in column 1.

    If column 1 does not have enough room to type the values, press F6.

    To insert a line, position the cursor in the first space of the Key column and press Enter. To delete a line, press Ctrl-F4.

8. Type any additional columns of corresponding values.

9. Press F10 to save the table and continue.

Lookup Table Function Keys:

Key	Function
F1	Help.
Shift-F2	Macros.
F4	Deletes cell entry.
Ctrl-F4	Deletes line.
Ctrl-F5	Auto-types current date.
Alt-F5	Auto-types current time.
F6	Expands field for long programs.
F10	Saves and continues.

Note

See *Lookup Statements* for an explanation of lookup tables and lookup statements.

Embedded Printing Commands

WRITE

Purpose

Enables you to change formats such as justification and line spacing as often as you want within a document. Also enables special features such as queued printing, date and time entry at time of printing, and printer pause.

Embedded Commands

Command	Meaning
*@DATE(*n*)*	Prints the date at the time of printing where *n* stands for one of the date format codes.
*@TIME(*n*)*	Prints the time at the time of printing where *n* stands for one of the time format codes.
JOIN filename	Queues printing with continuous page numbers, headers, and footers.
Justify No	Turns off right-margin justification.
Justify Yes	Turns on right-margin justification.
*LS*n*	Changes line spacing to *n* lines.
Printer code	Embeds printer command. Queues printing.
*QUEUEP *filename*	Queues printing with continuous page numbers.
Stop	Pauses printing at code's location in document so that you can change cartridges, etc. Press Enter to continue.

Export to ASCII

Purpose

Exports a Write document to an ASCII-format file.

To export to ASCII

1. Select **W**rite from the Main menu.

2. Select **U**tilities from the Write menu.

3. Select **E**xport A Document from the Utilities menu.

4. Select **A**SCII, **D**ocument ASCII, or **M**acintosh ASCII.

   Other options are D**C**A, **W**ordStar, Word**P**erfect, M**I**crosoft Word, M**U**ltiMate, and P**R**ofessional Write.

5. Type the ASCII file name and press **Enter**.

   The name must differ from the Write document's name.

Export options

- Select the **A**SCII option to export your document with carriage returns at the end of each line.

- Select the **D**ocument ASCII option to export your document with carriage returns at the end of each paragraph. The paragraphs must be separated by blank lines.

- Select the **M**acintosh ASCII option if you intend to exchange the file with a Macintosh user.

To export a Write document with headers, footers, and page numbers, see *Print A Document*.

External Lookup Statements

FILE

Purpose

Retrieves information from another Q&A database and inserts it into the current database.

External lookup statements

Use XLOOKUP statements to retrieve information you stored in other Q&A databases. The external database must be in the same directory or disk as the current database (or otherwise accessible to Q&A), unless you type all the necessary path information when you name the external data file.

An external lookup statement is analogous to a lookup statement, but it retrieves values from an external database rather than the current database's lookup table.

Note the following terms:

- **Primary file** is the current database in which the retrieved information will appear.

- **Primary key field** is the field of the primary file in which the retrieved information will be displayed. The name of this field must match the name of the external key field.

- **External file** is the database from which the information will be retrieved.

- **External key field** is a field of the external file that has exactly the same name as the primary key field.

- **Lookup field** is the field of the external file that contains the information to be retrieved.

You enter the external lookup statement in a field of the primary file, such as the primary key field. The statement says, in effect, "Look in the external file named such-and-such, and find a record in which the external key field's contents match what is typed in the primary key field. Then go to the lookup field on the same record, copy the information in that field, and display it here."

Suppose that you type a company's code name (AMAL) in the primary key field. You write an external lookup statement that retrieves the full company name from a database of company names. The name of the primary key field is "Company Name Code." The name of the external key field is also "Company Name Code." The external lookup statement tells Q&A to search the company name database for the record that contains the company name code "AMAL." It finds the record. This record has another field called "Company Name-Full." This field is the lookup field. Q&A retrieves the information from the lookup field and displays it in the current record.

External lookup operations occur when you add or update a data record and press F8 (Recalculate).

You must observe the following syntax when you create the LOOKUP statement:

> **XLOOKUP(***"primary file name", primary key field ID#, "external key field name", "lookup field name", destination field ID#***)**

Note that the field ID numbers do not require quotation marks, but all file names and field names do require quotation marks.

The following is a valid XLOOKUP statement:

> **#90:XLOOKUP("CNAMES",#90,"Company Name Code","Company Name_Full",#90)**

Note that this statement appears in field #90, employs this field as the primary key field, and places the retrieved information in this field. When you add data, the effect of such a statement is to replace the company code with the company full name when you press F8 or leave the record. You also can use other fields as the primary key field and destination field.

You must index the external key field for the external lookup function to work. For information on indexing fields, see *Speed Up Searches*.

An external lookup operation ignores uppercase and lowercase distinctions, but it returns the data with the capitalization pattern found in the external database.

Q&A has two XLOOKUP statements:

- XLOOKUP returns the corresponding value only when an exact match is found. If no exact match is found, Q&A just leaves the field blank.

- XLOOKUPR returns the corresponding value or, if no exact match is found, the next lower value in the external database.

An XLOOKUP statement retrieves only one field at a time, but you can use additional XLOOKUP statements to retrieve additional fields from the external database. These four statements all use the same primary key field (#90), but they retrieve information from four different lookup fields and place the information in four different destination fields. Type the company code in field #90, press **F8**, and Q&A does the rest.

> #90:XLOOKUP("CNAMES",#90,"Company Name Code","Company Name_Full",#90)

> #91:XLOOKUP("CNAMES",#90,"Company Name Code","Company Address",#91)

> #92:XLOOKUP("CNAMES",#90,"Company Name Code","Company State",#92)

> #93:XLOOKUP("CNAMES",#90,"Company Name Code","Company Zip",#93)

Before you use an external lookup statement, make sure that your CONFIG.SYS file contains the statement `FILES = 20` (or a higher value). From the DOS prompt, make the root directory current, then type **TYPE CONFIG.SYS** and press **Enter**.

To prepare the two databases

1. Design or redesign the files so that both have a field with the same name (such as "Company Name Code").

2. Use the **S**peed Up Searches option in the Customize menu to index the external key field in the external file.

3. Add data to the external file.

    Make a list of the code names you use so that you will remember how to type the codes in the primary file.

4. Place both databases in Q&A's directory to simplify retrieval.

To create an XLOOKUP or XLOOKUPR statement

1. Select **F**ile from the Main menu.

2. Select **D**esign File from the File menu.

3. Select **P**rogram A File from the Design menu.

4. Press **Enter** to confirm the file name.

5. Select **P**rogram Form from the Programming menu.

    Q&A displays the Program Spec screen.

6. Position the cursor in the field in which you want the external data value to appear.

7. Type a new field ID number (such as **#110**) followed by a colon (**:**).

8. Type **XLOOKUP** or **XLOOKUPR** and then type the following on one line, being careful to use exactly the punctuation that appears here. Press **F6** so you will have enough room.

    ("external filename",primary field ID#,"external key field","lookup field ", destination field ID#)

    Do not use quotation marks for field ID numbers.

9. Press **F10** to save your XLOOKUP statement and return to the File menu.

To look up data in an external database

1. Select **A**dd Data or **S**earch/Update from the File menu.

2. Type the name of the primary file.

    To see a list of available databases, press the space bar to clear the line and press Enter.

3. Position the cursor in the primary key field.

4. Type a key value or code that matches the key value or code you placed in the external key field of one of the records of the external file.

5. Press F8.

Notes

If you want to use the retrieved value in a formula, use an external lookup function rather than a lookup statement. See @XLOOKUP and @XLOOKUPR in *Functions* for information on using the lookup functions.

See *Lookup Statements* for information on looking up information from the current database's lookup table.

Field ID Number

FILE

Purpose

In form programming, assigns a unique number so the field can be referenced in formulas. You must assign a field ID number to each field you intend to mention in a Programming Statement.

To assign an identification number to a field

1. Select File from the Main menu.

2. Select Design File from the File menu.

3. Select Program A File from the Design menu.

4. Type the name of the database you want to program and press Enter.

5. Select Program Form from the Programming menu.

6. Position the cursor in the field to which you want to assign the identification number.

7. Type a pound sign (#) followed by a whole number.

   The number should not appear as an ID number anywhere else on the form.

8. Press **F10** to save the ID numbers and continue.

   See *Program Form* for information on writing program statements.

Note

Bear in mind that Q&A executes the programming statements in order; for example, Field #2 is executed before Field #5.

Font Assignments

WRITE

Purpose

Assigns your printer's fonts to the Regular and Font codes so that you can use them in your documents.

To install your printer's fonts

1. If you have not already done so, install your printer.

   Select **W**rite from the Main menu.

2. Select **T**ype/Edit from the Write menu.

3. Press **Ctrl-F9**.

4. Position the cursor in the Font File Name field and press **F6** to list the available files.

5. Use the arrow keys to select the correct font description file for your printer.

6. Move the cursor to the Regular field and press **Enter** to see a list of font options.

7. Use the **space bar** or arrow keys to select the font you want to use and press **Enter**.

8. Move the cursor to the next Font field and press **Enter** to see a list of font options.

9. Use the space bar or arrow keys to select the font you want to use and press Enter.

10. Repeat Steps 8 and 9 to assign up to 8 fonts.

11. Press F8 to make this Font Assignment screen the default for all documents.

   If you don't press F8, the assignment is valid for the current document only.

12. Press F10.

Fonts

WRITE

Purpose

Enhances text so that it prints with one of your printer's fonts.

To enhance text with fonts

1. Position the cursor at the beginning of the text you want to enhance.

   If you can't remember the number of the font you want to use, press Ctrl-F9 to display the Font Assignments screen before proceeding.

2. Press Shift-F6 to display the Enhancements menu.

3. Select Font.

4. Type the number of the font.

5. Use the arrow keys to select the text to enhance with the font you've chosen.

6. Press F10.

Note

To use fonts, you must install your printer and assign the fonts. See *Font Assignments* for more information.

Format Options

FILE

Purpose

Specifies how text and values display and print. Assign the formats using the database's Format Spec screen.

Note

You can use more than one code in a field. For instance, the code **N,4,C,JR** formats a number with four decimal places, commas, and right-justified.

Format Options

Code	Application
JR	Right-justifies **T**ext, **K**eywords, **N**umber, **D**ates, **H**ours, or **Y**es/no fields.
JC	Centers **T**ext, **K**eywords, **N**umber, **D**ates, **H**ours, or **Y**es/no fields.
JL	Left-justifies **T**ext, **K**eywords, **N**umber, **D**ates, **H**ours, or **Y**es/no fields.
U	Displays **T**ext, **K**eywords, or **Y**es/no fields with uppercase letters.
0-7	Specifies number of decimal digits.
C	Inserts commas in **N**umber and **M**oney fields.

Format Values

FILE

Purpose

Changes format options and information types in the Format Spec of the database.

To change the Format Spec for a database
1. Select **F**ile from the Main menu.

2. Select **D**esign File from the File menu.

3. Select **C**ustomize A File from the Design menu.

4. Type the file name and press **Enter**.

5. Select **F**ormat Values from the Customize menu.

   Q&A displays the Format Spec.

6. Press **Tab** repeatedly to select the field you want to change, then type the new codes.

7. Press **F10** until Q&A displays your database form again.

Note
See also *Design File*.

Functions

FILE

Purpose
Provides resources for constructing programming statements.

Q&A's Built-In Functions

@ABS(*n*)
A mathematical function that returns the absolute (positive) value of *n*.

@ADD
A context function that restricts execution of a programming statement to **A**dd Data. The statement does not function in **S**earch/Update.

@ASC(*x*)
A mathematical function that returns the ASCII decimal code of the first character of the string *x*.

@AVG(*list*)
A mathematical function that computes the average of the fields referenced in the *list*.

@CGR(*pv, fv, np*)
A financial function that computes the rate of return on an investment (*pv* = present value; *fv* = future value; *np* = number of periods).

@CHR(*ASCII code*)
A text/string function that returns the ASCII character equivalent of a decimal *ASCII code*).

@D(*date*)
A date/time function that enables the use of a *date* as a constant in a programming statement.

@DATE
A date/time function that returns the current date.

@DEL(*x,y,z*)
A text/string function that returns *x* with *z* characters deleted starting at character *y*.

@DITTO(*list*)
A text/string function in **A**dd Data that copies the values of the fields in the *list* from the preceding form to the new form.

@DOM(*n*)
A date/time function that returns an integer corresponding to the day of the date typed in field *n*.

@DOW(*n*)
A date/time function that returns the name of the day typed in field *n*.

@EXP(*x,y*)
A mathematical function that raises *x* to the *y* power.

@FILENAME
A text/string function that returns the name of the current data file.

@FV(*pa, i, np*)
A financial function that computes the future value of regular payments (*pa* = payment amount; *i* = interest; *np* = number of periods).

@HELP(*x*)
A text/string function that displays a custom Help screen for the field *x*.

@INSTR(*x,y*)
A text/string function that returns an integer showing the position (counting left to right) of string *y* in the text *x*.

@INT(*n*)
A mathematical function that returns the integer of *n*.

@LEFT(x,y)
A text/string function that returns the leftmost *y* characters of the string *x*.

@LEN(*x*)
A text/string function that returns the character length of the string in field *x*.

@LOOKUP(*key, column*)
A LOOKUP function that returns the corresponding value from the current data file's lookup table if an exact match is found and enables you to use the value in a programming statement. See *Lookup Statements* for an explanation of lookup tables and lookup procedures.

@LOOKUPR(*key, column*)
A LOOKUP function that returns the corresponding value from the current data file's lookup table if an exact match is found or returns the next lower value if an exact match is not found. Enables you to use the value in a programming statement. See *Lookup Statements* for an explanation of lookup tables and lookup procedures.

@MAX(*list*)
A mathematical function that returns the highest value in the *list* of referenced fields.

@MID(*x,y,z*)
A text/string function that returns *z* characters from the string *x* starting at position *y*.

@MIN(*list*)
A mathematical function that returns the lowest value in the *list* of referenced fields.

@MONTH$(*n*)
A date/time function that returns the name of the month in field *n*.

@MONTH(*n*)
A date/time function that returns an integer corresponding to the month of the date in field *n*.

@MSG(*x*)
A text/string function that displays the message *x* (maximum 80 characters) on the message line.

@NUM(*x*)
A mathematical function that returns the number found in the referenced field *x*, even if the field also contains text.

@NUMBER
A numbering function that returns a unique number that is one greater than the last @NUMBER entered.

@NUMBER(*n*)
A numbering function that returns a unique number that is *n* greater than the last @NUMBER(*n*) entered.

@PMT(*pv,i,np*)
A financial function that computes the amount of the periodic payment due on a loan (*pv* = present value; *i* = interest rate per period; *np* = number of payments).

@PV(*pa,i,np*)
A financial function that computes the present value of an annuity (*pa* = amount of periodic payment; *i* = interest rate per period; *np* = number of payments).

@RIGHT(*x,y*)
A text/string function that returns the rightmost *y* characters of *x*.

@ROUND(*x,y*)
A mathematical function that rounds the value *x* to *y* decimal places.

@SGN(*x*)
A mathematical function that returns an integer showing whether *x* is positive ($+1$), zero (0), or negative (-1).

@SQRT(*n*)
A mathematical function that returns the square root of *n*.

@STD(*list*)
A mathematical function that computes the standard deviation of the *list* of referenced fields.

@STR(*x*)
A text/string function that returns the text value of the number *x*.

@SUM(*list*)
A mathematical function that computes the sum of the *list* of referenced fields.

@T(*time*)
A date/time function that enables the use of a *time* as a constant in a programming statement.

@TEXT(*x,y*)
A text/string function that inserts *y* copies of the character or string *x*.

@TIME
A date/time function that returns the current time.

@UPDATE
A context function that restricts execution of a programming statement to Search/Update. The statement does not function in Add Data.

@USERID
A multiuser function that inserts the current user's ID number in the field.

@VAR(*list*)
A mathematical function that computes the variance of the *list* of referenced fields.

@WIDTH(*x*)
A text/string function that returns an integer that indicates the width of the field *x* (in characters).

@XLOOKUP(*filename, primary key field, external key field, lookup field*)
A function that searches an external file to match the value in the *primary key field* to a corresponding value in the *external key field*. If a match is found, returns the value in the *lookup field*.

@XLOOKUPR(*filename, primary key field, external key field, lookup field*)
A function that searches an external file to match the value in the *primary key field* to a corresponding value in the *external key field*. If a match is found, returns the value in the lookup field. If no match is found, returns the next lower value.

@YEAR(*n*)
A date/time function that returns an integer corresponding to the year of the date in field *n*.

Note

See also *Programming Statements*.

Get

Purpose

Retrieves a document from disk.

To retrieve a file from disk

1. Select **G**et from the Write menu.

2. Type the name of the document you want to retrieve and press **Enter**.

Note

When you retrieve a document with **G**et, it becomes the current document. Use **T**ype/Edit to display the document on-screen.

Global Format Options

Purpose

Changes global defaults for the display and printing of numbers, currency figures, times, and dates.

To change global format options

1. Select **F**ile from the Main menu.

2. Select **D**esign File from the File menu.

3. Select **C**ustomize A File from the Design menu.

4. Type the name of the database you want to customize and press **Enter**.

5. Select **F**ormat Values from the Customize menu.

6. Press **F10**.

7. In the Global Format Options screen, select the option you want to change. (Accept the default setting or press the left- or right-arrow keys to highlight another option.)

8. Repeat Step 7 to change other options.

9. Press **F10** after you finish changing options.

Notes

If you create fields with **N**umber, **M**oney, **D**ates, or **H**ours information types when you create a new database with **D**esign File, Q&A displays the Global Format Options menu.

See also *Date and Time Display*.

Go To

WRITE

Purpose

Moves the cursor to the specified page and line.

To move to a line or page you specify

1. Press **Ctrl-F7**.

2. Enter a page number and/or a line number.

Enter	*Cursor moves to*
Page and line number	The beginning of that line on that page.
Page number	The top of that page.
A line number	The beginning of that line, from the first line of the document.

To mark your current location, press **F5**.

3. Press **F10**.

To return to the original cursor location, press **Ctrl-F7**, then **Enter**.

Import Document

Purpose

Assists the user with retrieval of documents created with other word processing programs.

To retrieve a non-Q&A document from disk

1. Select Get from the Write menu.

2. Type the name of the document you want to retrieve and press Enter.

3. When the Q&A displays the Import Document menu, select ASCII, Special ASCII, Old WordStar, or Lotus 1-2-3 or Symphony.

Import Document options

- ASCII imports the document as a straight ASCII file, with carriage returns at the end of every line.

- Special ASCII imports the document as an ASCII file with carriage returns at the end of every paragraph.

- Old WordStar imports a WordStar file. Q&A converts the file to the Q&A format.

- Lotus 1-2-3 or Symphony imports a Lotus 1-2-3 or Symphony spreadsheet.

Note

Q&A can read the PFS:Write and IBM Writing Assistant file formats directly. If you retrieve a document with a file format other than those Q&A can read directly, you must identify the format.

Information Types

Purpose

Limits the type of information you can enter in a field.

To change information types in an existing database design

1. Select **F**ile from the Main menu.

2. Select **D**esign File from the File menu.

3. Select **R**edesign A File from the Design menu.

4. Type the data file name.

5. Press **F10**.

6. Press **Tab** repeatedly to select the field you want to change.

7. Type the new information type code.

8. Repeat Steps 6 and 7 for additional fields.

9. Press **F10** until Q&A displays the File menu.

Information Type Options

Option	*Application*
Text	Enables any character to be entered in the field.
Number	Limits input to numbers, commas, and decimal points.
Money	Formats numbers with dollar signs, commas, and two decimal places.
Keywords	Accepts keywords.
Dates	Accepts dates in three formats (June 20, 1990; 6/20/90; or 90-6-20) and reformats to the standard selected in the Global Format Options screen.
Hours	Accepts hours in several formats (such as 4 PM, 4:00pm, or 4pm) and reformats to the standard selected in the Global Format Options screen.

Option	Application
Yes/no	Accepts Yes, Y, True, T, or 1 for "yes," and No, N, False, F, or 0 for "no."

Notes

The default information type is Text. When you enter Number, Keywords, Dates, Hours (times), or Yes/no information in a field, override the default information type to prevent entering the wrong type of information.

See also *Design File* and *Redesign a File*.

Insert Document

WRITE

Purpose

Inserts an existing document into the current document at the cursor's location.

To insert a document at the cursor's location

1. Press F8 (Options).

2. Select Documents and press Enter.

3. Select Insert A Document and press Enter.

4. Type the name of the document you want to insert and press Enter.

Notes

You can insert any Q&A or imported document.

You also can insert documents using the printer command *JOIN*, but these inserted documents appear only in the printout. See *Embedded Printing Commands*.

Insert Mode

FILE, REPORT, ASSISTANT, WRITE

Purpose

Toggles the text entry/editing mode between the Overwrite and Insert modes.

To toggle Insert/Overwrite modes

Press **Ins**.

In Overwrite, the default mode, the characters you type erase existing text. In Insert mode, the characters you type do not erase existing text.

Justify

WRITE

Purpose

Turns on or off right-margin justification.

To turn on and off justification

1. In **T**ype/Edit, position the cursor where you want the justification to begin.

2. Type ***Justify Yes***. You can abbreviate this command to ***JYY***.

3. Position the cursor where you want the justification to end and type ***Justify No***. You can abbreviate this command to ***JYN***.

Notes

Justified text appears only on the printout.

You can justify the entire document by selecting Yes in the Justify option of the Print Options menu.

See also *Embedded Printing Commands*.

Keyword Reports

Purpose

Creates a report format in which keywords are listed in the first column and all records that contain the keyword are grouped in additional columns.

To create a keyword report

1. Select **R**eport from the Main menu.

2. Select **D**esign/Redesign A Report from the Report menu.

3. Type the name of the data file for which you are designing the report and press **Enter**.

4. Type a name for the report format and press **Enter**. The name can include up to 31 characters.

5. Select **C**olumnar or Crosstab (**X**) Report Type.

6. Select records you want to print with the Retrieve Spec screen. To print all records, press **F10**.

7. In the Column/Sort Spec screen, type **1,K** in the keyword field.

8. Add additional codes to indicate which fields to print as additional columns.

   Separate each code with a comma (**,**). If you run out of space in the field, press **F6** to expand the field.

9. Press **F10**.

10. Select print options and press **F10**.

11. Press **Y** to print the report or **N** to return to the Report menu.

Note

You must design your database to include at least one Keyword field (see *Design File* and *Information Types*) and enter semicolons (**;**) between each keyword.

Line Spacing

WRITE

Purpose

Sets line spacing.

To enter a line spacing code

1. Position the cursor on the line preceding the one with which you want the new line spacing to begin.

2. Type *LSn* where *n* is a whole number from 0 to 9.

Notes

To set line spacing for the whole document, enter the code at the beginning of the document (or set single or double line spacing by using the Print Options (WRITE) menu).

For more information on embedded commands, see *Embedded Printing Commands*.

Lookup Statements

FILE

Purpose

Retrieves information from the lookup table of the current database.

Lookup statements

Q&A has two LOOKUP statements:

- LOOKUP returns the corresponding value or, if no exact match is found, leaves the field blank.

- LOOKUPR returns the corresponding value or, if no exact match is found, the next lower value.

Use the following syntax when you type LOOKUP statements:

#n:LOOKUP(key, column, field ID#)

- *#n* is the field ID number of the field containing the lookup statement.

- *Key* is the value that you want Q&A to search for in the Key column of the lookup table.

- *Column* is the number of the lookup table column containing the corresponding value that you want Q&A to retrieve.

- *Field ID#* is the field where you want Q&A to enter the retrieved value.

To create a lookup table

1. Select **F**ile from the Main menu.

2. Select **D**esign File from the File menu.

3. Select **P**rogram A File from the Design menu.

4. Type the name of the data file you want to customize and press **Enter**.

5. Select **E**dit Lookup Table from the Programming menu.

   Q&A displays the lookup table screen for the current data file.

6. Type the key values in the Key column.

7. Type the corresponding values in column 1.

   If the column does not have enough room to type the values, press **F6**.

   To insert a line, position the cursor in the first space of the line in the Key column where you want to insert another line, then press **Enter**. To delete a line, press **Shift-F4**.

8. Type additional columns of corresponding values.

9. Press **F10** to save the lookup table and continue.

To create a LOOKUP or LOOKUPR statement

1. Select **F**ile from the Main menu.

2. Select **D**esign File from the File menu.

3. Select **P**rogram A File from the Design menu.

4. Type the name of the database you want to program and press **Enter**.

5. Select **P**rogram Form from the Programming menu.

6. Position the cursor in the field in which you want the corresponding value to appear.

7. Type a new field ID number (such as **#110**) followed by a colon (**:**).

8. Type **LOOKUP** or **LOOKUPR**, and indicate in parentheses the field ID# of the field where the lookup value is entered, the column from which the corresponding value is to be retrieved, and the field ID# of the field in which you want to display the retrieved value, as in the following example:

   LOOKUP(#9,1,#110)

   Press **F6** if you need to expand the field.

9. Press **F10** to save your LOOKUP statement.

Notes

You can type up to four columns of corresponding values, but Q&A retrieves only one corresponding value at a time.

If you want to use the corresponding value in a formula, use a LOOKUP function rather than a LOOKUP statement.

See *External Lookup Statements* for information on looking up information from other Q&A databases.

Macros

FILE, REPORT, WRITE

Purpose

Combines a sequence of functions into one command.

To define (or redefine) a macro

1. Press **Shift-F2**.

2. Select **D**efine Macro.

3. Press a key to identify the macro.

    Press any character, function key, or key combination using **Shift**, **Alt**, or **Ctrl**. You can use **Alt** key combinations with letters from the keyboard, such as **Alt-A**, and **Alt-B**.

4. Record the macro by performing the actions you want the macro to perform.

5. Press **Shift-F2** to turn off the macro recorder.

6. To save the macro to disk, press **Enter**. To retain the macro in memory only, press **Esc**.

To save macros in memory

1. Press **Shift-F2**.

2. Select **S**ave Macros.

3. To save macros to a generic macro file press **Enter**. To save to a different file, type the file name.

To play back a macro

Press the key you used to identify the macro.

To retrieve a macro file

1. Press **Shift-F2**.

2. Select **G**et Macros.

3. Type the name of the macro file and press Enter.

    To see a list of the macro files, press the **space bar,** then press **Enter**. Select the name of the macro file you want to use and press **Enter**.

To clear macro files from memory

1. Press **Shift-F2**.

2. Select **C**lear Macros.

Mail Merge

FILE, WRITE

Purpose

Generates personalized form letters by drawing data
from a File database and inserting that data into a Write
document.

To create a merge document

1. Type the text of the letter, but omit the specifics (such
   as name and address).

2. Position the cursor where you want to insert the field
   code and press **Alt-F7**.

3. Type the name of the database.

4. Highlight the field names you want to insert.

   To scroll through the list of field names, press **PgUp**,
   PgDn, **Home**, **End**, or the arrow keys.

5. Press **Enter**.

6. Repeat Steps 2 through 5 to add all the field codes
   you want to use.

   You can add **L**eft or **R**ight codes to control the
   spacing of the inserted data. Type the code before
   the closing asterisk (*).

7. Press **Shift-F8** to save your document.

To print a merge document

1. Display the merge document and press **F2**.

2. Press **Tab** to select the Name Merge File field, and
   accept or type the name of the database you are using.

3. Use the Retrieve Spec screen to retrieve only the
   documents you want to print.

   To print all the records, press **F10**. To sort the records
   before printing, press **F8**.

Note

After you create the merge document, you can print the
merge document with Write.

Mailing Labels

FILE, WRITE

Purpose

Generates mailing labels by drawing data from a File database and inserting the data into a Write document.

To create mailing labels

1. Select Mailing labels from the Write menu.

2. Select the name or size of your mailing labels.

3. Press F10.

    Q&A displays an on-screen simulation of the mailing label, with the field codes *First name*, *Last name*, *Address*, *City*, *State*, and *Zip* already inserted.

    To add additional codes, press Alt-F7 and type the name of the database. To see a list of available databases, press the space bar to clear the line and press Enter. Highlight the name of the database you want to use. Highlight the name of the field names you want to insert. Then press Enter. Repeat these Steps to add additional codes.

4. Press Shift-F8 to save your document.

To print mailing labels

1. Display the mailing label document and press F2.

2. Press Tab to select the name of the merge file field, then accept or type the name of the File database.

    Print first with the default settings; if you see problems, display the Mailing Label screen again and make the necessary changes.

3. Press F10.

4. Use the Retrieve Spec screen to retrieve only the documents you want to print. To print all the records, press F10. To sort the records before printing, press F8.

Note

> Q&A is designed to use commercial mailing labels from
> Avery, Moore, and others.

Mass Update

FILE

Purpose

> Makes changes to two or more forms at the same time.

To perform a mass update

1. Select **M**ass Update from the File menu.

2. Type the name of the database you want to update
   and press **Enter**.

   Q&A displays a Retrieve Spec screen.

3. Retrieve the records you want to update. (Press **F10**
   to retrieve all the records.)

   After you retrieve the records, Q&A displays the
   Update Spec screen.

4. Press **Tab** repeatedly to select the field you want to
   update.

5. Type a pound sign (**#**) and a unique number, followed
   by an equal sign (**=**).

   Because this number is different from the field ID
   numbers you assigned if you programmed the form,
   you can use those numbers again here.

6. Type the change. You can type text, a formula, or a
   conditional expression. (Remember to enclose text in
   quotation marks.)

7. Press **F10** to begin the update.

8. Press **Enter** to preview each confirmation before it is
   made; press **N**, then **Enter**, to update all the forms
   without confirmation.

   If you are confirming updates, press **Shift-F10** to
   confirm the update or **F10** to see the next record
   updating.

Newpage

WRITE

Purpose

Inserts a page break at the cursor location.

To force a new page

1. Position the cursor where you want the page break to occur.

2. Press F8 (Options).

3. Select Lay Out Page.

4. Select Newpage.

To delete a page break

Position the cursor on the page break symbol and press Del.

Operators

FILE

Purpose

Provides the symbols needed to express arithmetic, relational, and logical statements in form programs.

List of Operators

Operator	Purpose
+	Addition.
–	Subtraction.
*	Multiplication.
/	Division.
=	Equal to.
<	Less than.
>	Greater than.

Operator	Purpose
<=	Less than or equal to.
=>	Greater than or equal to.
<>	Not equal to.
AND	Both comparisons true.
OR	Either comparison true.
NOT	Reverses comparisons' values.

Order of Precedence

Operation	Precedence
division, multiplication	first
addition, subtraction	second
relational ($<, >, <=, =>, <>$)	third
logical (NOT)	fourth
logical (AND, OR)	fifth

Note

Q&A evaluates expressions according to rules of precedence (rather than left to right). You can override the precedence rules with parentheses. See *Program Form* and *Programming Statements*.

Print

FILE

Purpose

Produces printed output quickly and simply.

Notes

The Print command in the File menu lacks many of Report's sophisticated features, such as the capacity to sort records, print data in columns, perform calculations, and look up information in other Q&A databases.

For more information, see *Design/Redesign a Spec* and *Print Records.* To reset the default printing options, see *Set Global Options.*

Print a Document

WRITE

Purpose

Prints Write documents, including envelopes, merge documents, and mailing labels.

To print a document

1. To display a document that is not current, select Get from the Write menu.

2. Press F2.

3. Select print options.

4. Press F10 to begin printing.

Print Options

FILE, REPORT, WRITE

Purpose

Displays options for printing database output (File and Report) and documents (Write).

To select print options

1. Press Tab or the arrow keys to highlight the option you want to change.

2. Press the space bar or the arrow keys to highlight the setting you want to use or type the new value.

3. Repeat Steps 1 and 2 for additional options.

4. Press **F10** to start printing.

File and Report print options

- **Print to** routes output to one of five different printers or to disk or the screen.

- **Page preview** selects whether to display a page preview.

- **Type of paper feed** selects manual or continuous paper feed (and the bin from which paper is drawn, for multibin printers).

- **Print offset** offsets the page by a specified number of characters.

- **Printer control codes** turns on or off special features.

- **Print field labels** selects whether to include field labels.

- **Number of copies** specifies the number of copies.

- **Number of records per page** specifies the number of forms per page.

- **Number of labels across** selects the number of labels (up to 8) to print across the page.

Write print options

- **From page** specifies the page on which printing starts.

- **To page** specifies the page on which printing stops.

- **Number of copies** specifies the number of copies.

- **Print offset** specifies the position from which the print head starts printing.

- **Line spacing** sets single space or double space for the entire document. You also can select a special envelope setting. To change line spacing within a document, see *Line Spacing*.

- **Justify** specifies whether your document is justified. If you select justification, Write attempts to even the right margin by adding spaces between the words on a line.

- **Print to** sets up more than one printer or sets up a single printer with multiple modes. You also can print a fully formatted version of your document (complete with page numbers, headers, and pagination) to disk in ASCII format.

- **Type of paper feed** sets continuous or manual paper feed.

- **Number of columns** enables you to print up to eight columns on-screen. You do not see the columns until the document prints and you cannot change column spacing within the document. To change the spacing between columns (.25" by default), see *Set Global Options (WRITE)*.

- **Printer control codes** turn on or off special features.

- **Name of merge file.** For more information on this option, see *Mail Merge*.

File and Report Print Options Function Keys

Key	Function
F1	Provides Help.
F8	Goes to Define Page screen.
F10	Saves changes and prints.

Write Print Options Function Keys

Key	Function
F1	Provides Help.
Ctrl-F6	Displays Design Page screen.
F9	Saves changes and goes back without printing.
F10	Saves changes and prints.

Note

Your choices affect the current data file or document only. To change default Print Options, see Set Global Options.

Print Queuing

WRITE

Purpose

Organizes print jobs into one file that you can print at one time.

To print a series of documents

1. Select Clear from the Write menu.

2. To print a series of documents without continuous page numbers, embed the following commands in the blank document:

   *QUEUE *filename1**

   *QUEUE *filename2**

   *QUEUE *filename3**

   To print a series of documents with continuous page numbers, embed the following commands in the blank document. All of the files must include page numbers (see *Edit Header/Edit Foote*r).

   *QUEUEP *filename1**

   *QUEUEP *filename2**

   *QUEUEP *filename3**

   The *filenames* are the DOS file names of the documents you want to print.

To print a series of documents with continuous page numbers, headers, and footers

1. Use the Get command in the Write menu to load the first document.

2. Add headers, footers, and page numbering.

3. Position the cursor at the end of the document.

4. Type **filename**.

   The *filename* is the DOS file name of the document you want to join at the cursor's location.

5. Repeat Steps 3 and 4 to join additional documents.

6. Press F2 (Print) to proceed with printing.

Print Records

Purpose

Prints simple free-form printouts, coordinate printouts, and copies of forms as they appear on-screen.

To print all the records in the database, one per page

1. Select File from the Main menu.

2. Select Print from the File menu.

3. Select a file and press Enter.

4. Select Print Records from the Print menu.

5. Press F10 without selecting a Print Spec or typing a Print Spec's name.

6. Press F10 to select all the records.

7. Press F10 again to select all the fields.

8. Select print options.

   By default, Q&A does not print the field labels. To print the field labels, press Tab repeatedly to select Print Field Labels and select Yes.

9. Press F10 to start printing.

To print using a Print Spec you created

1. Select File from the Main menu.

2. Select Print from the File menu.

3. Select a file and press Enter.

4. Select Print Records from the Print menu.

5. Use the arrow keys to select a Print Spec or type the Print Spec's name. Then press F10.

6. Select No to use the Print Spec without changes or
   Yes to select the records or fields you want to print
   (see *Design/Redesign a Spec*).

7. Select print options.

8. Press F10 to start printing.

Note

For more complex printouts, see *Print Options*. To print
forms while adding or updating data, see *Single Form
Printing*.

Printer Codes

WRITE

Purpose

Enables control within a Write document of printer
special effects, such as condensed-mode printing,
expanded-mode printing, shadow-mode printing, or
near-letter quality mode printing.

To embed printer control codes in a document

1. Position the cursor where you want the special effect
   to begin.

2. Type *code1, code2, code3*.

   The *codes* are the ASCII decimal equivalents of the
   control codes used to turn on special effects.

3. Position the cursor where you want the special effect
   to end.

4. Type *code1, code2, code3*.

   The *codes* are the ASCII decimal equivalents
   of the control codes used to turn off special effects.

Note

To embed printer control codes in the text, type a
Write embedded command (see *Embedded Printing
Commands*). To find the printer's codes, consult your
printer's manual.

Printing Envelopes

Purpose

Finds the correspondent's address in a letter and prints the address on an envelope.

To print an envelope

1. Type the letter using centered text for the return address. Make the date the first left-justified line. Leave a blank line after the date and type the correspondent's address left-justified. Leave a blank line after the correspondent's address.

2. Insert an envelope in the printer. Line up the top of the envelope with the print head.

3. Press **F2**.

4. Use the down arrow to select Line Spacing.

5. Select Envelope.

6. Press **F10**.

   Write prints the address beginning eight lines down from the top of the envelope and indented 3 1/2 inches.

Program Form

Purpose

Displays the Program Spec screen so that you can create programming statements.

To access the Program Spec screen

1. Select **F**ile from the Main menu.

2. Select **D**esign File from the File menu.

3. Select **P**rogram A File from the Design menu.

4. Type the name of the database you want to program and press **Enter**.

5. Select **P**rogram Form from the Programming menu.

Program Spec Function Keys

Key	Function
F1	Displays how to program.
Shift-F2	Macros.
F3	Clears current spec.
F4	Deletes from cursor to end of field.
Shift-F4	Deletes all characters in field.
Ctrl-F5	Enters current date.
Alt-F5	Enters current time.
F6	Expands field for long programs.
F7	Goes to **S**earch/Update and displays Retrieve Spec screen.
F10	Saves and continues.

Note

See *Programming Statements* for more information.

Programming Statements

FILE

Purpose

Embeds instructions in fields to perform calculations using values from other fields, to look up values in the current database's lookup table or from separate Q&A databases, to move the cursor after the user finishes typing in a field, to instruct Q&A to execute an instruction only if a condition is met (see *Conditional Statements*), or to create complex statements that combine the above.

To create programming statements

1. Select **F**ile from the Main menu.

2. Select **D**esign File from the File menu.

3. Select **P**rogram A File from the Design menu.

4. Type the name of the database you want to customize and press **Enter**.

5. Select **P**rogram Form from the Programming menu.

6. Type field ID numbers in all fields to be referenced by the programming statement.

7. Type the programming statement in the field.

   To execute the statement when you move the cursor into the field, begin the statement with a less-than sign (**<**). To execute the statement when you move the cursor out of the field, begin the statement with a greater-than sign (**>**).

   If the statement that follows is a formula that returns a value you want to enter in the field, type an equal sign (**=**) followed by the rest of the statement. If the statement that follows is a LOOKUP statement, an external LOOKUP statement, a cursor-movement statement, or a conditional statement, type a colon (**:**).

   You can combine two or more programming statements by linking them with semicolons (**;**).

   If you run out of room to type the formula, press **F6** to expand the field.

8. Repeat Steps 6 and 7 to write additional programming statements.

9. To execute a statement upon entering or leaving a record, press **F8**, then type the entry field ID # and the exit field ID#, and then press **Enter**.

10. Press **F10** to save your programming statements and return to the File menu.

Notes

In manual recalculation mode (the default), programming statements are executed only when you press **F8** (Calculate). Press **Shift-F8** to select automatic recalculation mode, in which all statements are executed whenever the cursor leaves a field that has just been altered.

Except for fields specified as entry- or exit-calculation fields, Q&A calculates fields in the order of their field ID numbers.

Redesign a File

FILE

Purpose

Enables you to make changes to the database design even after data has been entered.

To redesign a database

1. Select **F**ile from the Main menu.

2. Select **D**esign File from the File menu.

3. Select **R**edesign A File from the Design menu.

4. Type the name of the database you want to redesign and press **Enter**.

   When the Design screen appears, you can change a label, lengthen or shorten an information blank, move a field, add a field, or delete a field.

5. Press **F10** to save the changes.

   If Q&A displays an error message, you shortened or deleted a field. Make sure that the changes will not truncate or lose valuable data. If you want to continue, press **F10**; otherwise, press **Esc**.

6. Change the information type or Format Spec of any field and define information types for any new fields.

7. Press **F10**.

   If your form has **N**umber, **M**oney, **D**ates, or **H**ours fields, Q&A displays the Global Format Options screen. Make any changes.

8. Press **F10**.

To redesign a file

1. Press **F8** to draw lines or boxes or to set new tabs before you add fields.

   To set tabs, select Set Tabs. To add lines or boxes, select Draw.

2. Position the cursor where you want a new field to appear.

3. Type the field label followed by a colon (**:**).

   If you want to limit the field length, insert the number of spaces by pressing the **space bar**. Then type a greater-than symbol (**>**).

   To create a multiline field, press **Enter** to leave blank lines. Then press **Tab** repeatedly to move the cursor to the right edge of the form and type a greater-than symbol (**>**).

4. Press **Tab** repeatedly or use the arrow keys to move to the next field's location.

5. Repeat Steps 2 through 4 to enter more fields.

6. Press **F10**.

7. Select an information type and format options for each field.

   The default information type is **T**ext, and the default format is Justify Left.

8. Press **F10**.

   If you select a **D**ates, **H**ours, **N**umber, or **M**oney information type, Q&A displays the Global Format Options screen. Change global formats for these fields or press **F10** to continue.

To change a label

1. Position the cursor on the label you want to change.

2. Press **Backspace**, **Del**, **F4**, or **Shift-F4** to delete text. Press **Ins** to insert text within the label.

To change a field length

1. Position the cursor within the information blank.

2. Press the space bar to add space or press Del to remove space. Type a greater-than symbol (>) where you want the field to end.

To move a field

1. Position the cursor on the first character of the field's label.

2. Press Shift-F5.

3. Highlight the label and codes and press F10.

4. Move the cursor to where you want the field and press F10.

To add a field

1. Press Ins.

2. Position the cursor where you want the new field to appear.

3. Type the field label, followed by a colon (:).

   You can use the less-than symbol (<) to define a rectangular multiline field or use the greater-than symbol (>) to define the end of the field.

To delete a field

Remove the field label and the field tag (codes such as AB or AC).

To change an information type

1. Perform editing tasks such as changing labels or moving fields.

2. Press F10 to display the Format Spec screen.

3. Type the new information type code. You also can change the Format Spec for each field.

   For lists of codes, see *Information Types* and *Format Options*.

4. Press F10 until Q&A displays the File menu.

Note

> Be careful not to alter the field tags (the internal codes such as AA, AB, or AC) that appear on the Design screen. If you accidentally delete one of the field tag characters, type the character back exactly the way it appeared. If you move or delete a field, be sure to move or delete the field tags too.

Remove

FILE

Purpose

> Deletes a group of data records from the database.

To remove records from the database

1. Select **R**emove from the File menu.

2. Type the name of the database from which you want to remove records and press **Enter**.

3. Type the search criteria.

   Remember to retrieve the records you want to delete, not the ones you want to keep!

4. Press **F10** to retrieve the records.

5. Press **Y** to confirm the deletion or **N** to cancel.

Note

> After you remove records you cannot retrieve them, so make a copy of the database and remove unwanted records from the copy.

Rename a Document

WRITE

Purpose

> Renames a Write document.

To rename a Write document

1. Select **W**rite from the Main menu.

2. Select **U**tilities from the Write menu.

3. Select **D**OS Facilities from the Utilities menu.

4. Select **R**ename A Document from the DOS Facilities menu.

5. Type the name of the file you want to rename and press **Enter**.

6. Type the new name and press **Enter**.

Rename/Delete/Copy a Spec

FILE

Purpose

Provides housekeeping functions for Print Specs.

To change the name of a Print Spec

1. Select **P**rint from the File menu.

2. Type the name of the database that contains the Print Spec you want to rename and press **Enter**.

3. Select **R**ename/Delete/Copy A Spec from the Print menu.

4. Select **R**ename A Print Spec from the Rename/Delete/Copy menu.

5. Type the Print Spec's present name and press **Enter**.

    If you do not remember the name, press **Enter** to see a list. Then press **F10** to continue.

6. Type the new name and press **Enter**.

To delete a Print Spec

1. Select **P**rint from the File menu.

2. Type the name of the database that contains the Print Spec you want to delete and press **Enter**.

3. Select **R**ename/Delete/Copy A Spec from the Print menu.

4. Select **D**elete A Print Spec from the Rename/Delete/Copy menu.

5. Type the Print Spec's present name and press **Enter**.

6. Press **Y** to confirm the deletion.

To use an existing Print Spec as the basis for another

1. Select **P**rint from the File menu.

2. Type the name of the database that contains the Print Spec you want to copy and press **Enter**.

3. Select **R**ename/Delete/Copy A Spec from the Print menu.

4. Select **C**opy A Print Spec from the Rename/Delete/Copy menu.

5. Type the name of the Print Specs you want to copy and press Enter.

6. Type the name of the new Print Spec and press **Enter**.

Restrict Values

FILE

Purpose

Customizes the database by restricting the range of values that can be typed into a field.

To restrict values

1. Select **F**ile from the Main menu.

2. Select **D**esign File from the File menu.

3. Select **C**ustomize A File from the Design menu.

4. Type the name of the database you want to customize and press **Enter**.

5. Select **R**estrict Values from the Customize menu.

6. Position the cursor on the field you want to restrict.

7. Type the value restriction symbol.

8. Type value restriction symbols in additional fields.

9. Press F10.

Value Restriction Options

Symbol	Function
x	Equal to x. Enables entry of exact match only.
$=x$	Equal to x. Enables entry of exact match only.
$/x$	Everything except x.
$/=$	Any field with data.
$x;y$	Enables entry of x or y.
$>x$	Greater than x. You cannot use this symbol in Yes/no fields.
$<x$	Less than x. You canot use this symbol in Yes/no fields.
$>=x$	Greater than or equal to x. You cannot use this symbol in Yes/no fields.
$<=x$	Less than or equal to x. You cannot use this symbol in Yes/no fields.
$x..y$	Begins with x and ends with y.
$>x..<y$	Greater than x and less than y. You cannot use this symbol in Yes/no fields.
?	A wildcard for any character. Use this symbol for Text and Keywords fields only.

Symbol	Function
..	Any number of characters. Use this symbol for Text and Keywords fields only.
x..	Begins with x. Use this symbol for Text and Keywords fields only.
..x	Ends with x. Use this symbol for Text and Keywords fields only.
x..y	Begins with x and ends with y. Use this symbol for Text and Keywords fields only.
..x..	Includes x. Use this symbol for Text and Keywords fields only.
..x..y..z..	Includes x, y, and z in that order. Use this symbol for Text and Keywords fields only.

Restrict Spec Function Keys

Key	Function
F1	Displays how to restrict values.
F6	Expands the field to make room for more symbols.
F10	Saves restrictions and continues.

Save

WRITE

Purpose

Saves the current document to disk.

To save your document

1. In Type/Edit, press Shift-F8 or select Save from the Write menu.

2. Type the name of the file. (If you previously saved the file, Q&A displays the file name on-screen.)

3. Press **Enter**. To exit the document, press **Esc**.

Search and Replace

WRITE

Purpose

Finds (and optionally replaces) a word or phrase in a Write document.

To perform a simple search

1. Press **F7**.

2. Type the search phrase.

   You can use the **?** and **..** wildcards. You also can search for formats using the **@** codes.

3. Press **F10**.

4. If a match is found, press **F7** to look for the next occurrence of the search phrase, edit the text, or press **Esc** to cancel the search. If no match is found, Q&A displays a message and the search is cancelled.

To repeat the last search

Press **F7** and **F10** to repeat the last search.

To perform a simple search and replace

1. Press **F7**.

2. Type the search phrase and press **Enter** or **Tab**.

3. Type the replacement text.

4. Press **F10**.

5. If a match is found, press **F10** to make the replacement, press **F7** to look for the next occurrence, or press **Esc** to cancel the search. If no match is found, Q&A displays a message and the Search and Replace operation is cancelled.

To perform a case-sensitive search or search and replace

1. Press **F7**.

2. Press **PgDn** to display the advanced features.

3. Press **Tab** repeatedly to select the Case option, then press the **space bar** to select Sensitive.

4. Press **Tab** repeatedly to select the Search For option, then type the search phrase. Be sure to type the exact pattern of capitalization you want to match.

5. If you want to perform a Replace operation, press **Enter** or **Tab** and type the replacement text next to the Replace With option.

6. Press **F10**.

7. If a match is found, press **F10** to make the replacement, press **F7** to look for the next occurrence, or press **Esc** to cancel the search. If no match is found, Q&A displays a message and the Search and Replace operation is cancelled.

To perform a search for part of a word

1. Press **F7**.

2. Press **PgDn** to display the advanced features.

3. Press **Tab** repeatedly to select the Type option, then press the **space bar** to select Text.

4. Press **Tab** repeatedly to select the Search For option, then type the search phrase. Be sure to type the exact pattern of capitalization you want to match.

5. If you want to perform a Replace operation, press **Enter** or **Tab** and type the replacement text next to the Replace With option.

6. Press **F10**.

7. If a match is found, press **F10** to make the replacement, press **F7** to look for the next occurrence, or press **Esc** to cancel the search. If no match is found, Q&A displays a message and the Search and Replace operation is cancelled.

To perform a search for a pattern

1. Press **F7**.

2. Press **PgDn** to display the advanced features.

3. Press **Tab** repeatedly to select the Type option, then press the **space bar** to select Pattern.

4. Press **Tab** repeatedly to select the Search For option, then type the search phrase.

   You can use the **9**, **a**, and ~ wildcards.

5. If you want to perform a Replace operation, press **Enter** or **Tab** and type the replacement text next to the Replace With option. You cannot use wildcards in replacement phrases.

6. Press **F10**.

7. If a match is found, press **F10** to make the replacement, press **F7** to look for the next occurrence, or press **Esc** to cancel the search. If no match is found, Q&A displays a message and the Search and Replace operation is cancelled.

To perform a forward or backward search

1. Press **F7**.

2. Press **PgDn** to display the advanced features.

3. Press **Tab** repeatedly to select the Range option, then press the **space bar** to select To End or To Beginning.

   Normally, Write searches the whole document. If you select To End, Write searches from the cursor to the end of the document. If you select To Beginning, Write searches from the cursor to the beginning of the document.

4. Press **Tab** repeatedly to select the Search For option, then type the search phrase. Be sure to type the exact pattern of capitalization you want to match.

5. If you want to perform a Replace operation, press **Enter** or **Tab** and type the replacement text next to the Replace With option.

6. Press **F10**.

7. If a match is found, press F10 to make the replacement, press F7 to look for the next occurrence or press Esc to cancel the search. If no match is found, Q&A displays a message and the Search and Replace operation is cancelled.

To perform a search and replace operation with automatic replacement

1. Press F7.

2. Press Tab repeatedly to select the Method option, then press the space bar to select Automatic or Fast Automatic. (The Automatic option displays each substitution as it is made, but Fast Automatic does not.)

3. Press Tab repeatedly to select the Search For option, then type the search phrase. Be sure to type the exact pattern of capitalization you want to match.

4. Press Enter or Tab and type the replacement text next to the Replace With option.

5. Press F10.

   If no match is found, Q&A displays a message and the Search and Replace operation is cancelled.

To perform a search and replace operation that removes a word

1. Press F7.

2. Press Tab repeatedly to select the Method option, then press B to select Automatic or Fast Automatic.

3. Press Tab repeatedly to select the Search For option, then type the search phrase. Be sure to type the exact pattern of capitalization you want to match.

4. Press Enter or Tab and type two periods (..) next to the Replace With option.

5. Press F10.

   If no match is found, Q&A displays a message and the Search and Replace operation is cancelled.

Wildcard Characters

Character	Meaning
?	Any single character.
..	Any number of characters.
9	Any single number.
a	Any single alphabetical character. To use this character, select Pattern in the Type option of the Search menu.
~	Any single nonalphanumeric character. To use this character, select Pattern in the Type option of the Search screen.

Format Codes

Code	Format
@BD	Boldface text enhancement.
@CR	Carriage return.
@CT	Centered line.
@F1	Font 1.
@F2	Font 2.
@F3	Font 3.
@F4	Font 4.
@F5	Font 5.
@F6	Font 6.
@F7	Font 7.
@F8	Font 8.
@IT	Italic text enhancement.
@NP	Hard page break (new page).

Code	Format
@RG	Regular text.
@SB	Subscript text enhancement.
@SP	Superscript text enhancement.
@UL	Underline text enhancement.
@XO	Strikeout text enhancement.

Search Options

FILE

Purpose

Tailors a Search/Update operation to retrieve documents that meet your search criteria.

To restrict searches

You can restrict searches in four ways:

- DO/ALL retrieves those forms that DO meet ALL the search restrictions you specify.

- DO/ANY retrieves those forms that DO meet at least one (ANY) of the search restrictions you specify.

- DO NOT/ALL retrieves those forms that DO NOT meet ALL of the search restrictions you specify.

- DO NOT/ANY retrieves those forms that DO NOT meet ANY of the search restrictions you specify.

To select records that DO NOT meet the restrictions

1. Select Search/Update from the File menu.

2. Type the name of the database and press Enter.

3. Press Ctrl-F7.

4. Use the arrow keys to highlight DO NOT, then press F10.

To select records that meet ANY of the restrictions

1. Select Search/Update from the File menu.

2. Type the name of the database and press Enter.

3. Press Ctrl-F7.

4. Use the arrow keys to highlight ANY, then press F10.

Note

ALL is the default when you type text or numbers to be matched in two or more fields. You can change the search logic so that ANY becomes the default temporarily, but ANY makes it harder to search for one record.

Search/ Update

FILE

Purpose

Retrieves records that meet criteria you specify. Provides an opportunity to edit, update, or add information on forms previously completed. You also can use Search/Update to delete unwanted records from the database.

To retrieve a single record

1. Select Search/Update from the File menu.

2. Type the name of the database and press Enter.

3. Type text that is unique to the data record you want to retrieve. To retrieve just the record you want, type text or numbers to be matched in more than one field. (The AND operator is the default.)

4. Press F10 to display the record.

   Update or edit the record.

5. Press Shift-F10 to save the changes and return to the File menu.

To search for one or more records

1. Select **S**earch/Update from the File menu.

2. Type the name of the database and press **Enter**.

3. Type search restriction options in one or more fields to retrieve records selectively. (The AND operator is the default.)

4. Press **F10** to display the records.

   Press **F9** and **F10** to go back and forth among the records you retrieve.

5. Press **Shift-F10** to save your changes and return to the File menu.

To retrieve all the records in the database

1. Select **S**earch/Update from the File menu.

2. Type the name of the database and press **Enter**.

3. Leave the Retrieve Spec screen blank and press **F10** to display all the records.

   Press **F9** and **F10** to go back and forth between the records you retrieve.

4. Press **Shift-F10** to save your changes and return to the File menu.

To delete an unwanted data record

1. Select **S**earch/Update from the File menu.

2. Type the name of the database and press **Enter**.

3. Type text that is unique to the data record you want to delete and press **F10** to display the record.

4. Press **F3** to delete the record.

5. Press **Y** to confirm the deletion.

6. Press **Shift-F10** to return to the File menu.

To print the form displayed on-screen

1. Press **F2**.

2. Select print options.

3. Press **F10** to start printing.

Search Restriction Options: All Information Types

Symbol	Explanation
x	Field must contain x.
$=x$	Field must contain x.
$/x$	Field can contain anything except x.
$=$	Field must be empty.
$/=$	Field must not be empty.

Search Restriction Options: All Information Types but Yes/No Fields

Symbol	Explanation
$x;y$	Field must contain x or y.
$x;y;z$	Field must contain x or y or z.
$>x$	Number must be greater than x.
$<x$	Number must be less than x.
$>=x$	Number must be greater than or equal to x.
$x..$	Number must be greater than or equal to x.
$..x$	Number must be less than or equal to x.
$<=x$	Number must be less than or equal to x.
$x..y$	Number must be in x to y range.
$>x..<y$	Number must be greater than x and less than y.
MAXn	Retrieves records with n highest values in field.
MINn	Retrieves records with n lowest values in field.

Search Restriction Options: Text and Keyword Fields

Symbol	*Explanation*
~	Retrieves words that sound alike.
?	Matches any single character.
\\	Matches literal character (performs case-sensitive search).
..	Retrieves anything from the periods to the end of the specification.
x..	Retrieves only if field begins with *x*.
..x	Retrieves only if field ends with *x*.
x..y	Retrieves only if field begins with *x* and ends with *y*.
..x..	Retrieves only if field includes *x*.
..x..y..z..	Retrieves only if field includes *x*, *y*, and *z*, in that order.

Search Restriction Options: Keyword Fields Only

Symbol	*Explanation*
x;y;z	Field must contain *x* or *y* or *z*.
&x,y;z	Field must contain *x* and *y* and *z*.

Search Restriction Options: Special Search

Symbol	*Explanation*
..	Retrieves records that contain correctly formatted data.
/..	Retrieves records that do not contain correctly formatted data.
]	In date fields only, matches the following text.

Search/Update Function Keys

Key	Function
F1	Provides Help.
F2	Prints current form.
Shift-F2	Macros.
Ctrl-F2	Prints from current form to end of stack.
F3	Deletes current record.
F4	Deletes from cursor to end of field.
Shift-F4	Deletes all characters in field.
F5	Dittos current field from preceding record.
Shift-F5	Dittos preceding record.
Ctrl-F5	Auto-types current date.
Alt-F5	Auto-types current time.
F6	Displays up to 17 records in 5-column table.
F7	Goes to Search/Update and displays Retrieve Spec screen.
F8	Calculates.
Shift-F8	Sets Calculation mode.
Ctrl-F8	Resets @NUMBER.
F9	Saves and displays preceding record.
Shift-F9	Goes to Customize Spec screen.
F10	Saves and displays a new, blank form.
Shift-F10	Saves record and exits.

Set Global Options

Purpose

Sets printing options for all the new Print Specs you create.

To change the print options defaults for all new Print Specs

1. Select Print from the File menu.

2. Type the name of the database you want to customize and press **Enter**.

3. Select Set Global Options from the Print menu.

4. To affect all new Print Specs, press **A** to select Change Print Options Defaults. To affect single-form printing output with **F2**, press **C** to select Change Single Form Print Defaults.

5. Press **Tab** repeatedly to select the option you want to change. For fields that require you to type something, select the field with **Tab** and type a response.

6. Press **F10** to save the options.

To change the define page defaults for all new Print Specs

1. Select Print from the File menu.

2. Type the name of the database you want to customize and press **Enter**.

3. Select Set Global Options from the Print menu.

4. To affect all new Print Specs for this database, press **B** to select Change Define Page Defaults. To affect single-form print output with **F2**, press **D** to select Change Single Form Page Defaults.

5. Press **Tab** repeatedly to select the option you want to change. For fields that require you to type something, select the field with **Tab** and type a response.

6. Press **F10** to save the options.

Print and page options

- **File Print Options** routes output, selects manual or continuous paper feed (as well as the bin from which paper is drawn, for multibin printers), offsets the page by the number of characters you specify (to leave room for binding), sends printer control codes to the printer to select features, includes or omits field labels, prints more than one copy, prints more than one form per page, and prints more than one label across the page.

- **Define Page** sets new page width, page length, and margins; the number of characters per inch to print; and whether to include headers and footers. Applies to print output generated by the Print Records command.

- **Single Form Print Defaults** displays the Print Options screen, but the choices apply to the single-form printing initiated by pressing F2 while adding or updating data.

- **Single Form Page Defaults** displays the Define Page screen, but the choices apply to the single-form printing initiated by pressing F2 while adding or updating data.

Notes

This command affects output generated by the Print command in the File menu. For more complex printing, see *Print Options*.

If you select Print Options and/or Define Page options, the choices you make affect all new Print Specs. For more information, see *Design/Redesign a Spec*.

Set Global Options

REPORT

Purpose

Redefines defaults for column headings and width, Report Format Options, Print Options, and Define Page options for all new report formats.

To change the column headings or width for all new reports for a particular database

1. Select **R**eport from the Main menu.

2. Select **S**et Global Options from the Report menu.

3. Type the name of the data file for which you are designing the report and press **Enter**.

4. Select Set **C**olumnar Global Options from the Global Options menu.

5. Select Set **C**olumn Heading/Widths from the Columnar Global Options menu.

6. Type the column width followed by a colon (**:**), then type the new column heading.

   To split the heading over two or more lines, type an exclamation point (**!**) where you want the split to occur.

7. Repeat Step 6 for additional columns.

8. Press **F10** to save your work and continue.

To change format options for all new report formats

1. Select **R**eport from the Main menu.

2. Select **S**et Global Options from the Report menu.

3. Type the name of the data file for which you are designing the report and press **Enter**.

4. Select Set **C**olumnar Global Options from the Global Options menu.

5. Select Set **F**ormat Options from the Columnar Global Options menu.

6. Press **Tab** repeatedly to select the option you want to change.

7. Press the **space bar** repeatedly to select the setting you want to use, then press **Enter**.

8. Repeat Steps 6 and 7 to select other options.

9. Press **F10** to save your work and continue.

To change print options for all new report formats

1. Select **R**eport from the Main menu.

2. Select **S**et Global Options from the Report menu.

3. Type the name of the data file for which you are designing the report and press **Enter**.

4. Select Set **C**olumnar Global Options from the Global Options menu.

5. Select Set **P**rint Options from the Columnar Global Options menu.

6. Press **Tab** repeatedly to select the option you want to change.

7. Press the **space bar** repeatedly to select the setting you want to use, then press **Enter**.

8. Repeat Steps 6 and 7 to select other options.

9. Press **F10** to save your work and continue.

To change define page options for all new report formats

1. Select **R**eport from the Main menu.

2. Select **S**et Global Options from the Report menu.

3. Type the name of the data file for which you are designing the report and press **Enter**.

4. Select Set **C**olumnar Global Options from the Global Options menu.

5. Press **D** to select Set Page Options from the Columnar Global Options menu.

6. Press **Tab** repeatedly to select the option you want to change.

7. Type the new value or press the **space bar** repeatedly to select the option you want to use, then press **Enter**.

8. Repeat Steps 6 and 7 to change other options.

9. Press **F10** to save your work and continue.

Columnar Global Options menu choices

The Columnar Global Options menu displays the following choices:

- **Set Column Headings/Width** enables you to type column headings and widths that differ from the labels in the database. Your choice affects all new report formats you create for the database.

- **Set Format Options** enables you to select new defaults for the spacing between columns, the repetition of values in sorted columns, and the treatment of blank fields and column breaks. Your choices affect all new report formats for all your databases.

- **Set Print Options** enables you to select new Report Print Options for new report formats for all databases.

- **Set Page Options** enables you to select new Define Page options, including headers or footers with page numbers and date and time, for new report formats for all your databases.

The choices you make with Set Global Options affect all new report formats.

Set Global Options

WRITE

Purpose

Changes editing, printing, and page definition defaults for all Write documents you create.

To set editing options

1. Select **W**rite from the Main menu.

2. Select **U**tilities from the Write menu.

3. Select **S**et Global Options from the Utilities menu.

4. Select Set **E**diting Options from the Global Options menu.

5. Select the field you want to change.

6. Select the option you want to use or type the value.

7. Repeat Steps 5 and 6 to select additional defaults.

8. Press **F10** to save your choices.

To change print defaults

1. Select **W**rite from the Main menu.

2. Select **U**tilities from the Write menu.

3. Select **S**et Global Options from the Utilities menu.

4. Select Change **P**rint Defaults from the Global Options menu.

5. Select the field you want to change.

6. Select the option you want to use or type the value.

7. Repeat Steps 5 and 6 to select additional defaults.

8. Press **F10** to save your choices.

To change the define page defaults

1. Select **W**rite from the Main menu.

2. Select **U**tilities from the Write menu.

3. Select **S**et Global Options from the Utilities menu.

4. Select Change Page **D**efaults from the Global Options menu.

5. Select the field you want to change.

6. Press **Tab** repeatedly to select the option you want to use or type the value.

7. Repeat Steps 5 and 6 to select additional defaults.

8. Press **F10** to save your choices.

To change import defaults

1. Select **W**rite from the Main menu.

2. Select **U**tilities from the Write menu.

3. Select **S**et Global Options from the Utilities menu.

4. Select Change **I**mport Defaults from the Global Options menu.

5. Select the field you want to change.

6. Press **Tab** repeatedly to select the option you want to
    use or type the value.

7. Repeat Steps 5 and 6 to select additional defaults.

8. Press **F10** to save your choices.

Global Options menu choices

The following list summarizes the options you can select
from the Global Options menu (the default settings are
shown in boldface type):

-   **Set Editing Options** enables you to change many
    word processing defaults: default editing mode
    (**Overtype**, Insert), default export type (**ASCII with
    CR**, ASCII without CR), automatic backup created
    when the document is loaded (Yes, **No**), decimal
    convention (**American**, European), show margins on
    screen (**Yes**, No), ghost cursor that tracks the cursor's
    location on the tab ruler (**Yes**, No), default tab
    settings (**5, 15, 25, 35** columns), and spacing between
    columns (**.25"**).

-   **Change Print Defaults** enables you to change many
    defaults: from page (**1**), to page (**End**), number of
    copies (**1**), print offset (**0**), line spacing (**Single**,
    Double, Envelope), justify (Yes, **No**), print to (**PtrA**,
    PtrB, PtrC, PtrD, PtrE, DISK), type of paper feed
    (Manual, **Continuous**, Bin1, Bin2, Bin3, Lhd),
    number of columns (**1**, 2, 3, 4, 5, 6, 7, 8), printer
    control codes (blank), and name of merge file (blank).

-   **Change Page Defaults** enables you to change many
    defaults: left margin (**10** columns), right margin (**68**
    columns from left edge of page), top margin (**6** lines
    from top), bottom margin (**6** lines from bottom), page
    width (**78** columns), page length (**66** lines), characters
    per inch (**10**, 12, 15, 17), begin headers/footers on
    page#: (**1**), and begin page numbering with
    page #: (**1**).

-   **Change Import Defaults** enables you to select
    page options for ASCII, WordStar, and Lotus
    imports.

The changes you make with Set Global Options affect
all new Write documents.

Set Global Options

Purpose

Sets defaults for the DOS location of Q&A document and database files, command execution, and network identification.

To change the default document and database directories

1. Use DOS to create subdirectories within Q&A's directory for databases and documents.

   If Q&A is in C:\QA, create subdirectories called C:\QA\DOCS and C:\QA\DATA.

2. Start Q&A and select **U**tilities from the Main menu.

3. Select **S**et Global Options and specify the directories where you want to store your data files and alternate program.

Notes

Keep your database and document files in directories other than Q&A's directory so that you cannot accidentally erase Q&A files while performing cleanup operations.

After you learn Q&A, select the option that executes commands when you press the command's letter.

Set Initial Values

Purpose

Fills in new forms with the most likely value or text. If the value or text is not correct, the user can change it when adding a new form.

To set initial values

1. Select **F**ile from the Main menu.

2. Select **D**esign File from the File menu.

3. Select **C**ustomize A File from the Design menu.

4. Type the name of the file you want to customize and press **Enter**.

5. Select Set **I**nitial Values from the **C**ustomize menu.

6. Type the initial value in the first field.

7. Press **Tab** to move to other fields and type initial values in those fields.

    To cancel the initial values for all fields in a form, press **F3**.

8. Press **F10** to save and continue.

Initial Values Spec Function Keys

Key	Function
F1	Displays how to set initial values.
F3	Cancels the Initial Values Spec in a form.
F10	Continues.

Single Form Printing

FILE

Purpose

Prints the form displayed on-screen.

To print the form displayed on-screen

1. Press **F2**.

2. Select print options.

3. Press **F10** to start printing.

Notes

You can print the form displayed on-screen or print all the forms you added during a data-entry session.

To select print options and page defaults for printing single forms, see *Set Global Options*.

Soft Hyphens

WRITE

Purpose

Inserts an optional hyphen, which Q&A uses only if
breaking the word improves the appearance of the line.

To add a soft hyphen

Position the cursor on the character before which you
want to insert the soft hyphen and press **Alt-F6**.

Sort

FILE

Purpose

Arranges records according to defined sorting criteria.

To sort all the records in the database

1. Select **S**earch/Update from the File menu.

2. Type the name of the database and press **Enter**.

3. Press **F8**.

4. Position the cursor in the first sort field and press **1**.

   To select an ascending sort, type **AS.** To select a
   descending sort, type **DS**.

5. Position the cursor in the next sort field and type the
   number one whole number larger than the preceding
   number. (In the second field, press **2**.) Then type **AS**
   or **DS**.

6. Repeat Step 5 using successive numbers.

7. Press **F10** to start the sort.

Search/Update Function Keys

Key	Function
F1	Provides /Help.
F2	Prints current form.
Shift-F2	Macros.
Ctrl-F2	Prints from current form to end of stack.
F3	Deletes current record.
F4	Deletes from cursor to end of field.
Shift-F4	Deletes all characters in field.
F5	Dittos current field from preceding record.
Shift-F5	Dittos preceding record.
Ctrl-F5	Auto-types current date.
Alt-F5	Auto-types current time.
F6	Displays up to 17 records in 5-column table.
F7	Goes to Search/Update and displays Retrieve Spec screen.
F8	Calculates.
Shift-F8	Sets Calculation mode.
Ctrl-F8	Resets @NUMBER.
F9	Saves and displays preceding record.
Shift-F9	Goes to Customize Spec screen.
F10	Saves and displays a new, blank form.
Shift-F10	Saves record and exits.

Notes

You can define two or more sort levels. The first sort level arranges all the records in ascending or descending order. The second sort level deals with records whose order cannot be determined with the first sort level.

After you sort the records, you can edit, update, add to, or delete the records, just as you do in Search/Update.

Speed Up Searches

FILE

Purpose

Creates a presorted index of frequently-searched fields to search large databases faster or to make sure that a field contains a unique entry or a nonunique entry.

To access the Customize menu

1. Select File from the Main menu.

2. Select Design File from the File menu.

3. Select Customize A File from the Design menu.

4. Type the name of the file you want to customize and press Enter.

To mark a field for automatic indexing

1. Select Speed Up Searches from the Customize menu.

2. Position the cursor in the field you want to index and press S.

3. Repeat Step 2 for additional fields.

4. Press F10 to save your choices.

To make sure a field contains a unique entry

1. Select Speed Up Searches from the Customize menu.

2. Position the cursor in the field you want to index and type SU.

3. Repeat Step 2 for additional fields.

4. Press F10 to save your choices.

To make sure a field contains a nonunique entry

1. Select **S**peed Up Searches from the Customize menu.

2. Position the cursor in the field you want to index and type **SE**.

3. Repeat Step 2 for additional fields.

4. Press **F10** to save your choices.

Note

You can index 115 fields, but each index uses disk space.

Summary Functions

REPORT

Purpose

Returns column totals, subtotals, averages, and other statistics which can be used in derived column formulas.

Summary Functions

@TOTAL(*n*)
Returns the total of values in column *n*.

@TOTAL(*n,m*)
Returns the subtotal of values in column *n* where a break occurs in column *m*.

@AVERAGE(*n*)
Returns the average of values in column *n*.

@AVERAGE(*n,m*)
Returns the subaverage of values in column *n* where a break occurs in column *m*.

@COUNT(*n*)
Returns the total count of values in column *n*.

@COUNT(*n,m*)
Returns the subcount of values in column *n* where a break occurs in column *m*.

@MINIMUM(*n*)
Returns the lowest value in column *n*.

@MINIMUM(*n,m*)
Returns the lowest value in column *n* where a break occurs in column *m*.

@MAXIMUM(*n*)
Returns the highest value in column *n*.

@MAXIMUM(*n,m*)
Returns the highest value in column *n* where a break occurs in column *m*.

Note

Summary functions can be used only in the Derived Columns screen.

Table View

FILE

Purpose

Displays up to 17 records at a time in table form.

To display a Table View of the entire database

1. Select Search/Update from the File menu.

2. Type the name of the database and press Enter.

3. Leave the Retrieve Spec screen blank and press F10 to display the records.

4. Press Alt-F6 to display the Table View.

   Q&A displays the first five fields in table form. Each column contains the first 20 characters of a field.

5. To display a complete record, use the arrow keys to highlight the record and press F10.

To select the fields that appear in the Table View mode

1. Select Search/Update from the File menu.

2. Type the name of the database and press Enter.

3. Leave the Retrieve Spec screen blank and press F10 to display the records.

4. Press Shift-F6 to display the Table View Spec screen.

5. Position the cursor in the field you want to appear in column 1, and press 1.

6. Position the cursor in the field you want to appear in column 2, and press 2.

7. Continue until you have selected all fields you want to include in Table View.

8. Press F10 to see the customized Table View.

Cursor-Movement Keys in Table View

Key	Cursor Movement
Up arrow or F9	Moves to preceding row.
Down arrow or space bar	Moves to next row.
Left arrow or Right arrow	Displays additional fields.
F10	Moves to current record.
Home	Moves to top of current display screen.
End	Moves to bottom of current display screen.
Ctrl-Home	Moves to first row in table.
Ctrl-End	Moves to last row in table.
PgUp	Moves to preceding 17 rows.
PgDn	Moves to next 17 rows.

Tabs

FILE, WRITE

Purpose

Overrides the default tab stops

To change tabs

1. Press **F8** (Options).

2. Select Lay Out Page, then select Set Tabs.

3. Press the right- or left-arrow keys to position the cursor on the tab line.

4. Press **T** for a left-justified **T**ab or **D** for a **D**ecimal tab.

   With decimal tabs, characters are entered right-justified until you type a period (decimal point); then the characters align normally.

   To delete an existing tab stop, position the cursor on the tab and press **Del**.

5. Repeat Steps 3 and 4 to set additional tabs.

6. Press **F10** to save the changes with the file.

Note

To change the default tab settings for all documents, see *Set Global Options*.

Temporary Margins

Purpose

Temporarily indents text from the left and right margins.

To indent text left and right

1. Position the cursor on the column in which you want the left- or right-indent to occur and press **F6**.

2. Select **L**eft margin or **R**ight margin indentation.

   The left margin change begins on the line below the current cursor position, and the right margin change begins on the current line. Q&A displays right and left brackets on the ruler line to mark the temporary margins.

3. Type the text to be indented.

   If you are indenting text in an existing document, the indentation takes effect for the current paragraph only. If you are typing new text, the indentation continues to the next paragraph.

To remove temporary indentations

Position the cursor within the indented text, press F6, then select Clear.

Text Enhancements

WRITE

Purpose

Formats characters with boldface, italics, subscript, superscript, underline, strikeout, and printer fonts.

To select text enhancements

1. Type the text you want to enhance.

2. Move the cursor to the first character of the text you want to enhance.

3. Press Shift-F6.

4. Select Boldface, Underline, SuPerscript, Subscript, Italics, Strikeout (X), Regular, or a font.

5. Highlight all the text you want to enhance.

6. Press F10.

To restore normal text

Highlight the text, press Shift-F6, and select Regular. Then press F10.

Note

See *Font Assignments* and *Fonts*.

Type/Edit

Purpose

Creates a new document or permits editing of the document currently in memory.

Type/Edit Function Keys

Key	Function
F1	Displays Help menu.
Shift-F1	Checks spelling (document).
Ctrl-F1	Checks spelling (word).
Alt-F1	Thesaurus.
F2	Prints document.
Shift-F2	Defines macro.
Ctrl-F2	Prints block.
F3	Deletes block.
Ctrl-F3	Document statistics.
F4	Deletes word (Ctrl-T).
Shift-F4	Deletes line (Ctrl-Y).
Ctrl-F4	Deletes to end of line.
F5	Copies block.
Shift-F5	Moves block.
Ctrl-F5	Copies block to file.
Alt-F5	Moves block to file.
F6	Sets temporary margins.
Shift-F6	Enhances text.
Ctrl-F6	Defines page.
Alt-F6	Soft hyphen.

Key	Function
F7	Searches and replaces.
Shift-F7	Restores deletion or makes multiple copies.
Ctrl-F7	Goes to a specific page or line.
Alt-F7	Lists fields.
F8	Options menu.
Shift-F8	Saves document.
Ctrl-F8	Exports document.
Alt-F8	Prints mailing labels.
F9	Scrolls screen up.
Shift-F9	Scrolls screen down.
Ctrl-F9	Font assignments.
Alt-F9	Calculates.
F10	Continues.

Note

To edit an existing document, use Get before Type/Edit.

Index

G-I

J-K